MOS Study Guide for Microsoft® Office 365

John Pierce

PUBLISHED BY
Microsoft Press
A Division of Microsoft Corporation
One Microsoft Way
Redmond, Washington 98052-6399

Library of Congress Control Number: 2012940331
ISBN: 978-0-7356-6903-1

Printed and bound in the United States of America.

First Printing

Microsoft Press books are available through booksellers and distributors worldwide. If you need support related to this book, email Microsoft Press Book Support at mspinput@microsoft.com. Please tell us what you think of this book at http://www.microsoft.com/learning/booksurvey.

Acquisitions and Developmental Editor: Rosemary Caperton
Editorial Production: Waypoint Press
Technical Reviewer: Jorge Diaz
Copyeditor: Roger LeBlanc
Indexer: Christina Yeager
Cover: Jelvetica

Contents

Taking a Microsoft Office Specialist Exam vii

    Microsoft Office Specialist Certification vii

    Selecting a Certification Path vii

    Test-Taking Tips viii

    Certification Benefits. ix

    For More Information. x

Using This Book to Study for a Certification Exam. x

    Office 365 Releases and This Book. xi

    Features and Conventions of This Book. xi

How to Get Support and Provide Feedback xii

    Errata & Book Support xii

    Getting Help with Microsoft Office 365 xii

    We Want to Hear from You xiii

    Stay in Touch xiii

Exam 77-891 Microsoft Office 365 Specialist

    What You Need to Know 1

1   **Navigating Office 365**   **3**

    1.1 Navigate Office 365 Features 3

        Understanding Office 365 Authentication 4

        Working on the Office 365 Home Page. 4

        Configuring Office 365 to Work with the Office Desktop Applications 9

        Getting Started with Outlook Web App 11

        Viewing Your Team Site 13

        Updating Your Profile 16

        Getting Help and Support 18

What do you think of this book? We want to hear from you!

Microsoft is interested in hearing your feedback so we can continually improve our books and learning resources for you. To participate in a brief online survey, please visit:

microsoft.com/learning/booksurvey

1.2 Navigate Office 365 Applications 26

    Using the Outlook Navigation Pane. 26

    Navigating on Your Team Site. 30

Objective Review. 32

2   Communicating by Using Office 365 Outlook Web App   33

2.1 Manage E-mail. 33

    Creating and Sending Messages. 34

    Reviewing and Replying to Messages 37

    Searching and Filtering Your Message Store. 41

    Working with Attachments 44

    Using Inbox Rules 45

2.2 Organize Calendars 50

    Recording Appointments. 50

    Working with Meeting Requests. 52

    Using the Scheduling Assistant 55

    Setting Up Shared Calendars and Managing Permissions 56

    Publishing Calendars. 58

    Adding Calendars 60

    Using Categories, Flags, and Reminders 60

    Switching Calendar Views. 64

2.3 Manage Contacts 65

    Adding Contacts 65

    Editing Contact Information 67

    Deleting a Contact. 67

    Forwarding Contact Information 67

    Creating Groups and Distribution Lists 68

    Importing Contacts. 71

    Searching Contacts 72

2.4 Manage Tasks 73

    Creating Tasks. 73

    Updating Task Information. 76

    Marking Tasks Complete 77

2.5 Configure Outlook Web App Options. 78

    Viewing Account Options. 78

    Organizing E-mail 80

    Using Groups 83

Changing Outlook Settings 83
Using Your Mobile Phone with Outlook Web App .86
Blocking or Allowing Messages. 88
Objective Review 90

3   Collaborating by Using Lync Online   91

3.1 Configure Lync Options 91
General Page 92
Personal Page. 93
Status Page 94
My Picture Page. 94
Phones Page. 95
Alerts Page 96
Ringtones And Sounds Page 96
Audio Device Page 97
Video Device Page. 97
File Saving Page 98
3.2 Employ Collaboration Tools and Techniques 100
Holding Group Conversations 100
Holding Web Conferences 109
Sending Instant Messages 112
Audio Conferencing 115
Setting Up a Video Conference. 115
3.3 Manage Lync Contacts. 117
Using Contact Groups. 117
Specifying Contact Relationships 119
Managing Status and Presence Settings 121
Managing Activity Feeds 123
Viewing Conversation History. 123
3.4 Use Lync Tools 126
Using Recording Manager 126
Using the Always On Top Option 128
Taking Notes in OneNote. 128
Changing the Conversation Subject. 129
Objective Review 130

4   Managing Sites in SharePoint Online   131

4.1 Search for Site Content 132

Setting a Search Scope 132

Using Advanced Search 133

Working with Search Results 135

4.2 Manage Sites 136

Using Tags and Notes 136

Working with Your My Site Profile 139

Sharing Your Site 141

Working with Groups and Permissions 141

Creating a Site Template 146

Using List Templates 147

Applying a Site Theme 148

Changing the Appearance of a List 149

Creating a Site 150

4.3 Manage Site Content 154

Selecting the Library You Need 154

Managing Library Views 156

Working with Library Settings 161

Using a Document Library 166

Using a Wiki Page Library 180

Creating Pages 181

Working with Lists 182

Working Offline with Content on Your Team Site 189

Objective Review 191

Index   193

What do you think of this book? We want to hear from you!

Microsoft is interested in hearing your feedback so we can continually improve our books and learning resources for you. To participate in a brief online survey, please visit:

microsoft.com/learning/booksurvey

Taking a Microsoft Office Specialist Exam

Desktop computing proficiency is increasingly important in today's business world. As a result, when screening, hiring, and training employees, employers can feel reassured by relying on the objectivity and consistency of technology certification to ensure the competence of their workforce. As an employee or job seeker, you can use technology certification to prove that you already have the skills you need to succeed, saving current and future employers the trouble and expense of training you.

Microsoft Office Specialist Certification

Microsoft Office Specialist certification is designed to assist employees in validating their skills with Microsoft Office applications, including Word, Excel, PowerPoint, Outlook, Access, and OneNote, as well as SharePoint and Office 365. The following certification paths are available:

- A Microsoft Office Specialist (MOS) is an individual who has demonstrated proficiency by passing a certification exam in one or more Microsoft Office applications, including Word, Excel, PowerPoint, Outlook, Access, and OneNote, as well as SharePoint and Office 365. The exam for Office 365 covers objectives for skills you need to work in Outlook Web App, Microsoft Lync, and SharePoint Online.
- A Microsoft Office Specialist Expert (MOS Expert) is an individual who has taken his or her knowledge of Office 2010 to the next level and has demonstrated by passing a certification exam that he or she has mastered the more advanced features of Word 2010 or Excel 2010.

Selecting a Certification Path

When deciding which certifications you would like to pursue, you should assess the following:

- The program and program version(s) with which you are familiar
- The length of time you have used the program and how frequently you use it
- Whether you have had formal or informal training in the use of that program

- Whether you use most or all of the available program features
- Whether you are considered a go-to resource by business associates, friends, and family members who have difficulty with the program

Candidates for MOS-level certification are expected to successfully complete a wide range of standard business tasks, such as formatting a document or worksheet and its content; creating and formatting visual content; locating information in a notebook; communicating with coworkers through Lync; or working with SharePoint lists, libraries, and Web Parts. Successful candidates generally have six or more months of experience with a specific Office application, including either formal, instructor-led training or self-study using MOS-approved books, guides, or interactive computer-based materials.

Candidates for MOS Expert-level certification are expected to successfully complete more complex tasks that involve using the advanced functionality of the program. Successful candidates generally have at least six months, and may have several years, of experience with the programs, including formal, instructor-led training or self-study using MOS-approved materials.

Test-Taking Tips

Every MOS certification exam is developed from a set of exam skill standards (referred to as the objective domain) that are derived from studies of how the Office 2010 programs or SharePoint are used in the workplace. Because these skill standards dictate the scope of each exam, they provide critical information about how to prepare for certification. This book follows the structure of the published exam objectives; see "Using This Book to Study for a Certification Exam" later in this book for more information.

The MOS certification exams for Microsoft Office 2010 applications, as well as SharePoint and Office 365, are performance based and require you to complete business-related tasks in the program for which you are seeking certification. You might be told to adjust program settings or be presented with a file and told to do something specific with it. Your score on the exam reflects how well you perform the requested tasks within the allotted time.

Here is some helpful information about taking the exam:

- Keep track of the time. You have 50 minutes to complete the exam. Your exam time does not officially begin until after you finish reading the instructions provided at the beginning of the exam. During the exam, the amount of time remaining is shown at the bottom of the exam interface. You can't pause the exam after you start it.

- Pace yourself. At the beginning of the exam, you will be told how many questions are included in the exam. Some questions will require that you complete more than one task. During the exam, the number of completed and remaining questions is shown at the bottom of the exam interface.

- Read the exam instructions carefully before beginning. Follow all the instructions provided in each question completely and accurately.

- Enter requested information as it appears in the instructions, but without duplicating the formatting unless you are specifically instructed to do so. For example, the text and values you are asked to enter might appear in the instructions in bold and under-lined text, but you should enter the information without applying these formats.

- Close all dialog boxes before proceeding to the next exam question unless you are specifically instructed not to do so.

- Don't close task panes before proceeding to the next exam question unless you are specifically instructed to do so.

- If you are asked to print a document, worksheet, chart, report, or slide, perform the task, but be aware that nothing will actually be printed.

- Don't worry about extra keystrokes or mouse clicks. Your work is scored based on its result, not on the method you use to achieve that result (unless a specific method is indicated in the instructions).

- If a computer problem occurs during the exam (for example, if the exam does not respond or the mouse no longer functions) or if a power outage occurs, contact a testing center administrator immediately. The administrator will restart the com-puter and return the exam to the point where the interruption occurred, with your score intact.

Certification Benefits

At the conclusion of the exam, you will receive a score report, indicating whether you passed the exam. You can print with the assistance of the testing center administrator. If your score meets or exceeds the passing standard (the minimum required score), you will be contacted by email by the Microsoft Certification Program team. The email message you receive will include your Microsoft Certification ID and links to online resources, including the Microsoft Certified Professional site. On this site, you can download or order a printed certificate, create a virtual business card, order an ID card, view and share your certification transcript, access the Logo Builder, and access other useful and interesting resources, including special offers from Microsoft and affiliated companies.

Using the Logo Builder, you can create a personalized certification logo that includes the MOS logo and the specific programs in which you have achieved certification. If you achieve MOS certification in multiple programs, you can include up to six of them in one logo.

Microsoft Access 2010 Certified
Microsoft Excel 2010 Certified
Microsoft Outlook 2010 Certified
Microsoft PowerPoint 2010 Certified
Microsoft Word 2010 Certified

You can include your personalized logo on business cards and other personal promotional materials. This logo attests to the fact that you are proficient in the applications or cross-application skills necessary to achieve the certification.

For More Information

To learn more about the Microsoft Office Specialist exams and related courseware, visit:

www.microsoft.com/learning/en/us/certification/mos.aspx

Using This Book to Study for a Certification Exam

The Microsoft Office Specialist (MOS) exams for individual Microsoft Office 2010 applications, as well as SharePoint and Office 365, are practical rather than theoretical. You must demonstrate that you can complete certain tasks rather than simply answering questions about program features. The successful MOS certification candidate will have at least six months of experience using all aspects of an application on a regular basis; for example, using Outlook Web App at work to send messages, track contact information, schedule appointments and meetings, track and assign tasks, and take notes.

Each chapter in this book is divided into sections addressing groups of related skills. Each section includes review information, generic procedures, and practice tasks you can complete on your own while studying. You can practice the procedures in this book by using your own files.

As a certification candidate, you probably have a lot of experience with the program you want to become certified in. Many of the procedures we discuss in this book will be familiar to you; others might not be. Read through each study section and ensure that you are familiar with not only the procedures included in the section, but also the concepts and tools discussed in the review information. In some cases, graphics depict the tools you will use to perform procedures related to the skill set. Study the graphics and ensure that you are familiar with all the options available for each tool.

Office 365 Releases and This Book

Microsoft updates Office 365 regularly. To learn about exciting new features and improvements to Office 365, see *http://community.office365.com/en-us/w/office_365_service_updates/default.aspx*. This study guide was written during the spring of 2012 and is based on the E3 edition of the midsize and enterprise plan. It covers the certification exam scheduled to be released in summer 2012.

Features and Conventions of This Book

While covering the objectives and skills described in this book, you can use the detailed table of contents to scan a listing of the topics covered in each chapter and locate specific topics.

You can save time when you use this book by understanding how special instructions, keys to press, buttons to click, and other conventions are indicated in this book.

Convention	Meaning
1 2	Numbered steps guide you through step-by-step procedures.
→	An arrow indicates a procedure that has only one step.
See Also	These paragraphs direct you to more information about a given topic in this book or elsewhere.
Tip	These paragraphs provide a helpful hint or shortcut that makes working through a task easier, or information about other available options.
Interface elements	In procedures, the names of program elements (such as buttons and commands) are shown in bold characters.
Key combinations	A plus sign (+) between two key names means that you must hold down the first key while you press the second key. For example, "press Ctrl+Home" means "hold down the Ctrl key and press the Home key."
User input	In procedures, anything you should enter appears in bold italic characters.

How to Get Support and Provide Feedback

The following sections provide information on errata, book support, feedback, and contact information.

Errata & Book Support

We've made every effort to ensure the accuracy of this book and its companion content. Any errors that have been reported since this book was published are listed on our Microsoft Press site at oreilly.com:

http://go.microsoft.com/FWLink/?Linkid=250941

If you find an error that is not already listed, you can report it to us through the same page.

If you need additional support, please send an email message to Microsoft Press Book Support at *mspinput@microsoft.com*.

Please note that product support for Microsoft software is not offered through the addresses above.

Getting Help with Microsoft Office 365

If your question is about Microsoft Office 365 and not about the content of this Microsoft Press book, your first recourse is the Microsoft Office 365 Help system or community forums. Detailed information about how to access and use the Office 365 Help system and other resources is covered in Chapter 1, "Navigating Office 365."

If your question is about Office 365 or another Microsoft software product and you cannot find the answer in the product's Help system, please search the appropriate product solution center or the Microsoft Knowledge Base at:

support.microsoft.com/

In the United States, Microsoft software product support issues not covered by the Microsoft Knowledge Base are addressed by Microsoft Product Support Services. Location-specific software support options are available from:

support.microsoft.com/gp/selfoverview/

We Want to Hear from You

At Microsoft Press, your satisfaction is our top priority, and your feedback our most valuable asset. Please tell us what you think of this book at:

www.microsoft.com/learning/booksurvey/

The survey is short, and we read *every one* of your comments and ideas. Thanks in advance for your input!

Stay in Touch

Let's keep the conversation going! We're on Twitter: *http://twitter.com/MicrosoftPress.*

Microsoft Office 365 Specialist

In this book's four chapters, you'll build on the skills required to work collaboratively and on your own in Microsoft Office 365. The objectives covered in this study guide are directed toward readers who use Office 365 at the feature and functionality level. This study guide is not a comprehensive guide to how to administer Office 365 for a small business or in a larger organization. In using this study guide, you'll learn more about the specific skills you need to be certified as a Microsoft Office 365 specialist. The general areas covered are the following:

- Navigate the Office 365 home page and applications
- Work with Outlook Web App to send and manage e-mail messages, calendar appointments and meetings, contacts, and tasks
- Use Microsoft Lync 2010 to conduct online meetings and conferences with colleagues and contacts, including how to use audio, video, and screen sharing
- Manage and share documents, libraries, and lists using a SharePoint team site and how to manage your profile in your My Site

What You Need to Know

Individuals, small businesses, and large organizations uses Office 365 through a program of subscriptions and licenses. You can find details about the different subscription plans available at *www.office365.com*. (On that site, you can also subscribe to a 30-day trial of Office 365.)

Currently, Office 365 is offered under two general plans, one for small businesses and one for midsize businesses and enterprises. (You can choose between two different plans for a midsize and enterprise subscription.)

Individuals who sign up for Office 365 have administrative privileges, which lets them manage user accounts and licenses, for example. Office 365 administrators can also manage general settings for Outlook Web App, Lync, and SharePoint Online. In the Office 365 enterprise plans, administrators also manage security groups, deployment, and a large array of other settings that integrate Office 365 with the organization's network. The Office 365 Help system provides specific topics for administrators, and administrators can also find more information about Office 365 at *http://technet.microsoft.com/en-us/library/hh852576.aspx*.

For the most part, the descriptions and screen shots in this study guide are based on the Office 365 E3 plan for midsize businesses and enterprises. When possible, differences between this plan and the P1 plan for small businesses are noted. In addition to the wider range of administrative tasks required to deploy and manage Office 365 in a midsize or large organization, many of the differences between the small business plan and the enterprise plans reside in the default appearance and level of functionality available in the SharePoint Online team site that comes with Office 365. The team site in the small business plan is based on the Express Team Site template. In the enterprise plans, the site is based on the standard SharePoint Team Site template.

Administrator privileges are not required to complete most of the procedures and practice tasks in this study guide. However, to work through the procedures and practice tasks in Chapter 4, "Managing Sites in SharePoint Online," readers should be set up as an Office 365 administrator, be a member of the Team Site Owners group, or be granted Full Control permission to the site directly. If you are not an Office 365 administrator, you should ask someone who is to give you the necessary permissions to have full control of the team site. (An administrator can create a separate team subsite for you to practice on if necessary.)

Chapter 1, "Navigating Office 365," begins with a description of Office 365 features, including how to sign in to the Office 365 portal home page. Before you begin working through this guide, you should purchase an Office 365 subscription, obtain Office 365 credentials (user name and password) from an administrator in your organization, or sign up for one of the free, 30-day Office 365 trials.

> **Important** For information about updates to Office 365, see "Office 365 Releases and This Book" at the beginning of this book.

1 Navigating Office 365

The skills tested in this section of the Microsoft Office exam for Office 365 relate to how you navigate features and applications. You'll learn about navigating on the home page, in Outlook Web App, and on your team site in SharePoint Online. Specifically, the following objectives are associated with this set of skills:

1.1 Navigate Office 365 features

1.2 Navigate Office 365 applications

In this chapter, you'll gain an understanding of how Office 365 integrates its features, the navigational tools it provides on the home page, and the options you have for finding help and support. You'll also be introduced to working with the navigation pane in Outlook Web App and how to use the Quick Launch and breadcrumbs to navigate on your SharePoint team site.

Office 365 features and navigation are described at a high level in this chapter. In the following three chapters, you'll find detailed descriptions of how you work with specific Office 365 applications.

1.1 Navigate Office 365 Features

You gain access to the applications and features that Office 365 provides on a portal page that you open in your web browser. After you sign in to the portal, you work with the type of user interface controls (mostly links) that you find on most any other website. This section describes the features you work with in Office 365 and how you navigate to them from the portal's home page. You'll learn, for example, about resources and community sites you can rely on to help you set up your Outlook contacts and e-mail account. This section also describes the basic functionality of Outlook Web App and the SharePoint team site. In addition, you'll see how to view and update your profile and learn about the help and support features for Office 365.

Understanding Office 365 Authentication

Like many applications, Office 365 requires you to sign in using an ID and password. If you sign up for Office 365 (for yourself or for your organization), these authentication credentials are issued to you as part of that process. If you did not sign up yourself but are part of a small business or an organization that has deployed Office 365, you likely received your ID and a temporary password from the person responsible for administering Office 365. When you sign in the first time using the temporary password, you are required to reset that password.

> **Tip** Use a strong password for your Office 365 account. A strong password includes a mix of uppercase and lowercase letters, numbers, and special characters (such as a dollar sign or an underscore). You can learn more about creating strong passwords at *http://www.microsoft.com/security/online-privacy/passwords-create.aspx.*

> **See Also** For information about changing your password at other times, see "Updating Your Profile" later in this chapter.

Instead of having a Windows Live ID that you use to sign in to Hotmail or other Windows Live services, you need a Microsoft Online Services ID to work with Office 365. In a basic deployment of Office 365, you can recognize this ID because it includes the text *onmicrosoft* as part of the domain name you generally use for your e-mail address—for example, sam@contoso.onmicrosoft.com. (If you are using Office 365 on a custom domain instead of the domain set up by Microsoft, your user ID might not include this text.)

Working on the Office 365 Home Page

You can open the Office 365 portal in a couple of ways. Both approaches require you to sign in with your Microsoft Online Services ID and password.

Using *portal.microsoftonline.com*

To go directly to the sign-in page that takes you to the Office 365 portal, open your web browser and then type **https://portal.microsoftonline.com** in the address bar. (Of course, you might want to add this site to your list of favorites or create a shortcut to the site because you are likely to visit the site often.) Enter your user ID and password, and then click Sign In. Select Remember Me if you want to access the portal without having to enter your user ID. (You still need to enter your password.) The option Keep Me Signed In lets you close your browser but remain signed in to Office 365 until you manually sign out.

> **Important** Microsoft recommends that you select the Keep Me Signed In option only when you are working on a private computer. It's not advisable to select this option if you are working with Office 365 on a public computer or on a computer you share with others.

You sign in with your Microsoft Online Services ID and password. Microsoft provides this ID when you sign up for Office 365, or you might receive it from an administrator.

As you can see in the following screen shot, the home page of the Office 365 portal organizes links and information in two panes and a top navigation bar. Links to applications and websites appear on the left and at the top, and links to resources and community sites are included in a list at the right.

> **Important** Users who are Office 365 administrators see the Admin page when they sign in (and the Admin link appears in the top navigation bar). The Admin page includes additional links, such as those for managing Office 365 applications; accessing support sites; and managing users, subscriptions, and licenses.

The Office 365 home page for a standard user of the enterprise plan. Use the links at the top to open Outlook or your team site. Use the search box or the links under Community to find help and support.

Several of the resource links lead to information about setting up Outlook Web App. For example, you can read how to import your contacts into the address book in Outlook Web App and how to connect the Web App to the desktop version of Microsoft Outlook. (Compatible versions are Outlook 2007 with service pack 2, Outlook 2010, and Outlook 2011 for the Mac. Note that Outlook 2007 and Outlook 2010 require updates that are installed when the desktop setup is completed.)

> **See Also** You'll learn the details of how to import contacts in Chapter 2, "Communicating by Using Office 365 Outlook Web App." You'll learn more about setting up Outlook to work with Office 365 in "Configuring Office 365 to Work with the Office Desktop Applications" later in this chapter.

One Office 365 application you might not be familiar with is Microsoft Lync. Lync is a real-time communications application that provides capabilities for instant messaging, online meetings (using Voice over IP, or VoIP), and displaying presence information that tells you when a colleague is available or busy.

> **See Also** You'll learn the details of working with Lync in Chapter 3, "Collaborating by Using Lync Online."

Lync isn't installed by default. To install it, click Install Lync to open the Downloads page. (You can reach the same destination by clicking Downloads in the list of resources.) Specify whether you want to install the 32-bit or 64-bit version of Lync, and then click Install.

> **Important** The version you choose depends on which version of the Windows operating system you are using. Click the Which Version link to learn more about determining which version of Lync to use.

After the installation of Lync is complete, you should see the Lync window, where you sign in to the program using your Microsoft Online Services ID and password. You might need to install the Microsoft Online Services Sign-in Assistant if it is not already installed on your computer. If that's the case, you'll see a message in the Lync window when you try to sign in telling you that you need to install additional software. Click the message to download the installation file you need.

Microsoft Lync is a real-time communications application that you can use for instant messaging, online meetings, conference calls, and other needs.

On the portal's home page, the links under Community take you to online forums and blogs that are one of the support options for Office 365. You can also use the search box above the Resources list to find information about a topic. You'll learn more about Office 365 help and support later in this section.

➤ **To display the Office 365 portal**

1. Open your browser, and then type **https://portal.microsoftonline.com** in the address bar.

2. Enter your user ID and password, and then click **Sign in**.

➤ To install Lync

1. Sign in to the Office 365 portal.

2. On the home page, click **Install Lync**.

3. On the **Downloads** page, specify whether you want to install the 32-bit version of Lync or the 64-bit version.

4. Click **Install**.

Using Office365.com

An alternative route to the portal is to open the Office 365 product website, *office365.com*, and sign in there. (The Sign In link appears in the top-right corner of the page. This link takes you to the sign-in page shown earlier in this chapter.)

On this site, you can find information about Office 365, including current subscription plans. The Office 365 site also provides background information (such as customer stories and overviews of Office 365 features), links to sites where you purchase a subscription or download the free trial, and links to support sites.

Click Sign In in the top-right corner of the Office 365 product website to sign in and open the portal for work.

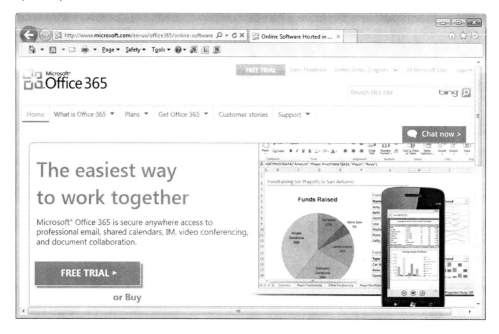

➤ **To sign in to the portal from www.Office365.com**

1. Open your browser, and then type **www.Office365.com** in the address bar.

2. At the top right of the Office 365 site, click **Sign In**.

3. On the Office 365 sign-in page, enter your user ID and password, and then click **Sign In**.

Configuring Office 365 to Work with the Office Desktop Applications

On the Downloads page you use to install Lync, you'll also find options to install Microsoft Office Professional Plus (an option that is provided only in the enterprise version of Office 365) and for configuring Office 365 so that it works with the Office desktop applications.

If you are not already running the Professional Plus edition of Office 2010 and want to install it, select 32-Bit or 64-Bit under Version, and then click Install. Use the links provided to get more information about installing and upgrading to this edition and to determine which version you should install.

As the information on the Downloads page indicates, by configuring the Office desktop applications to work with Office 365, you can send e-mail from Outlook 2007 or Outlook 2010 and save files to your SharePoint team site when you are working in an application such as Microsoft Word or Microsoft Excel.

In this area, click the Set Up button to start the process. Click Run in the security dialog box, and you'll then see Office 365 download the setup file it needs to configure the desktop applications. Sign in to Office 365 when you are prompted. At this point, the setup program checks your current configuration and then opens a page, shown in the following screen shot, that describes the steps the program will take and which applications it can configure.

Configuring Outlook 2007 or Outlook 2010 to work with Office 365 requires manual steps. Other configuration requirements are performed automatically.

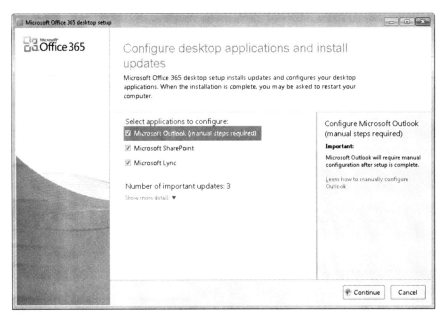

Be sure to take note of the information that tells you that configuring Outlook requires some manual steps. (The steps for connecting your account to Outlook 2010 are summarized later in this section.) If you want to review the steps involved before you proceed, click the link provided. Also note that the setup program might need to install updates to your computer. Use the Show More Details link to see a list of the updates.

If you don't want to configure a particular application, clear the check box. Click Continue after you specify the options you want to use, and then click I Accept if you agree with the licensing terms. The setup program then downloads the updates and configures the applications.

After the updates are installed, you are prompted to restart your computer to complete several of the configuration steps. When your computer restarts, the Office 365 desktop setup program should run again and complete the configuration steps it performs automatically. These steps include adding a shortcut for Office 365 to the Start menu and setting up SharePoint to work with the desktop applications.

To finish configuring Outlook, review the steps and other information described in the Help topic that is displayed when you click the link Learn How To Manually Configure Outlook. For Outlook 2010, you take the following steps:

1. Open Outlook 2010.
2. Click the **File** tab. On the **Info** page, click **Add Account**.

3. In the **Add New Account Wizard**, on the **Auto Account Setup** page, type your name and your Office 365 e-mail address, and then enter and confirm your password in the text boxes provided.

4. Click **Next**.

   With the information you provided in step 3, Outlook should automatically find the other settings it needs and complete the setup of your account.

5. Restart Outlook to have the new settings take effect.

➤ **To set up and configure Office desktop applications to work with Office 365**

1. On the Office 365 portal home page, click **Downloads** in the **Resources** list.

2. On the **Downloads** page, under **Set up and configure your Office desktop apps**, click **Set Up**.

3. Sign in to Office 365 when prompted.

4. In the Office 365 desktop setup program, select the Office applications you want to configure, and then click **Continue**.

5. Restart your computer when you are prompted.

6. Follow the steps required to set up your Office 365 account in Outlook 2007 or Outlook 2010. See the steps provided earlier in this section for Outlook 2010. You can also click **Connect Outlook** on your desktop in the **Resources** list on the Office 365 home page to find more information.

Getting Started with Outlook Web App

Outlook Web App (sometimes abbreviated OWA) is the online version of the desktop e-mail, scheduling, and contact-management application. Outlook Web App includes four views—Mail, Calendar, Contacts, and Tasks. This configuration is essentially the same as what's available in the desktop version.

> **See Also** If you want to read a comparison of the features available in Outlook Web App and the desktop version of Outlook, go to *http://help.outlook.com/en-US/beta/ Cc511379.aspx*.

At the top of the portal's home page, click Outlook to open your inbox. Under the Outlook heading in the portal's main pane, click Inbox, Calendar, or Options to start working in a particular view of Outlook Web App. The Inbox and Calendar links take you to the views in Outlook that you use for e-mail and for scheduling, respectively. The Options link takes you to a page on which you can change or set options to manage your e-mail accounts and calendar. For example, from the Options page you can connect different e-mail accounts, organize aspects of e-mail such as rules and automatic replies, join and manage e-mail groups, and control many aspects of how you want Outlook to behave.

> **See Also** You'll learn the details of working with these options in Chapter 2.

As mentioned earlier, several of the links in the Resources list on the home page direct you to procedures and information that help you set up Outlook Web App—importing contacts and connecting to your desktop version of Outlook.

The Account view of the Outlook Options page also includes a list of shortcuts. Click these links to display pages on which you start and complete the operations described.

Open the Outlook Web App Options page to view account information and configure settings.
Use the shortcuts to help set up and manage your e-mail account.

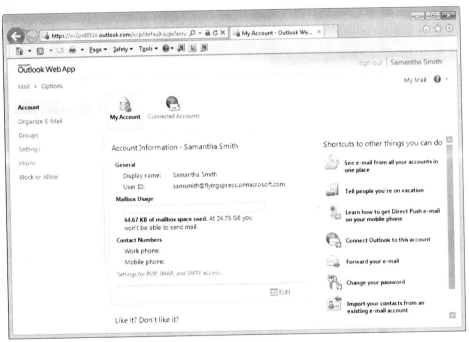

When you run Outlook Web App the first time (by clicking the Inbox link, for example, or by clicking Outlook at the top of the home page), you see a dialog box that prompts you to specify the language and time zone you want to use. After you choose settings and click OK in this dialog box, Outlook Web App opens.

➤ To get started with Outlook Web App

1. Sign in to the Office 365 portal.

2. On the home page, click **Outlook** at the top of the page.

3. Specify a language and time zone, and then click **OK**.

Viewing Your Team Site

The Office 365 team site is built on the Microsoft SharePoint platform. Organizations, teams, and groups use SharePoint sites as tools for collaborative needs such as managing shared content, tracking tasks, posting announcements, and managing business workflows.

> **Important** In the enterprise version of Office 365, users who are not set up as Office 365 administrators do not have access to the team site until an administrator adds them as a user of the site.

On the Office 365 portal home page, clicking Team Site in the top navigation bar opens the team site in the window in which the portal is displayed. You can click the Back button in your browser to return to the portal home page. Click Visit SharePoint Home in the Team Site section of the main pane to open the team site in a new window.

Use links on the home page to open the SharePoint Online team site. This screen shot shows the basic framework you will build from.

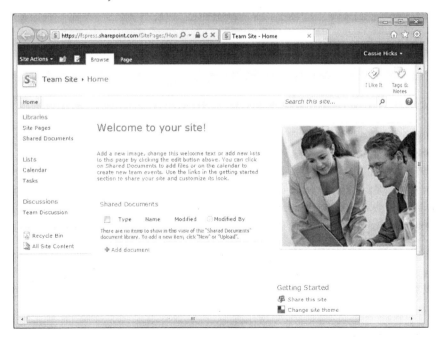

Two of the main elements of a SharePoint site are libraries and lists, both of which you use as repositories for information. If you have sufficient permissions for the team site, you can, for example, create a document library for each project your team manages or define a library in which you store specific types of documents—proposals, budgets, presentations, reports, and so on. You can also create other types of libraries, including picture libraries for storing image files and wiki page libraries, which are designed for sharing information within a group.

You start in this dialog box when you add libraries, lists, and pages to your team site. Filter the view by selecting categories at the left.

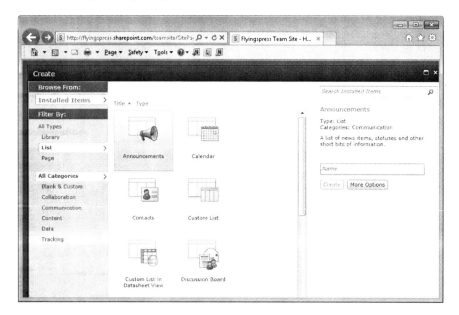

Lists are designed for specific uses—tracking tasks, for example, or listing announcements or contacts. Your team site can also include subsites. (Again, only users with sufficient permissions can create subsites.) A business might use the main team site as its intranet home page, and then each department could develop its own subsite, which it uses to store and display content relevant to its work and role within the business at large.

With the Office 365 enterprise or small business edition, you can implement the three-state workflow. (The enterprise version of Office 365 includes other types of workflows as well.) This workflow lets you track an item through three phases, or states. For example, you could track a request for proposal (RFP) through states named Submitted, Pending, and Approved.

See Also For more information about site permissions, working with SharePoint features such as lists and libraries, and using Office Web Apps with SharePoint, see Chapter 4, "Managing Sites in SharePoint Online."

The Small Business Edition Team Site and Website

In the small business edition of Office 365, the team site is configured differently from how it appears in the enterprise edition. The Office 365 home page for the small business edition, for example, contains a link to a default document library (Shared Documents). It also contains icons that run the Office Web Apps for Word, Excel, PowerPoint, and OneNote. The documents you create by using these icons are stored in the default Documents library.

The team site's home page is also configured differently. It contains links you can use to edit the home page, add new pages, and share the site with others. It also provides a list for posting announcements.

The basic team site for the small business version of Office 365.

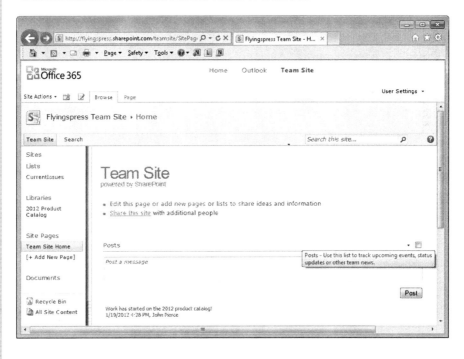

In addition, the portal home page for the small business edition includes a link to a public website that is built using SharePoint features. This site contains five standard pages—Home, About Us, Contact Us, Site Map, and Member Log In. To edit this page, you must be an Office 365 administrator.

If you are an administrator, click Admin on the portal's home page, and then click Edit Website. You'll see a SharePoint document library that stores the five default pages. You can change the look and feel of the website, add pages and images, and modify other properties of the site by using the tools on the ribbon that appears when you edit a page. You can apply much of what you learn about SharePoint sites in Chapter 4 to design your public site.

Updating Your Profile

An Office 365 profile includes information such as your name, country or region, and e-mail address. The fields in the Information area—First Name, Address, and Phone Number, for example—only display data. You cannot edit this information yourself on this page. An Office 365 administrator enters some of this information when your account is set up and can update this information when necessary.

The My Profile page includes a setting for the display language you want to use and, for Office 365 administrators (in the enterprise plan), contact preferences—that is, the contact information you want Microsoft Online Services to use to contact you. You can enter phone and e-mail address information and also select options for the type of information you want to be contacted about. For example, you can choose to receive (or not receive) educational content about how to set up and use products and services.

As part of your profile, you can choose to receive information about Office 365.

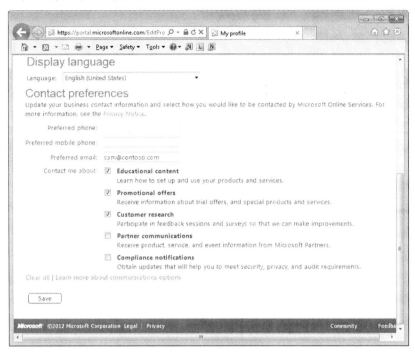

If you want to include a photograph of yourself in your profile, click Change Photo, click Browse to select an image file on your computer or network (or type the file name along with the path to the file), and then click Upload. The photo you add cannot be more than 100 kilobytes (KB) in size.

Another operation you perform on the My Profile page is changing your password. Click the link near the top of the page. At this point, you might need to sign in again for security reasons. You then follow the standard steps for defining a new password—enter your old password and then enter and confirm your new password. The Change Password page indicates how strong your password is—that is, whether your password uses a healthy mix of uppercase and lowercase letters, numerals, and symbols.

To view your profile and make any changes to your password, photo, or contact preferences, click My Profile in the top-right corner of the portal's home page. Make any changes, and then click Save.

➤ To change your password

1. On the portal page, click **My profile**.
2. On the **My profile** page, click **Change password**.
3. Sign in to Office 365 when prompted.
4. Type your current password. Type your new password, and then enter your new password again to confirm it.
5. Check the **Password Strength** indicator to be sure you are using a strong password.
6. Click **Submit**.

➤ To add or change a profile photo

1. On the portal page, click **My profile**.
2. On the **My profile** page, click **Change photo**.
3. Click **Browse**.
4. In the **Choose File to Upload** dialog box, select the image file you want to use, and then click **Open**.
5. On the **My profile** page, click **Upload**.

Getting Help and Support

When you have a question about how to work with Office 365, you can take several routes toward the answer. First, you can use the search box on the portal home page to locate information about a topic. The search results open in a new window and include topics from the Office 365 Help system as well as information from community forums. On the search results page, use the links below the search box (All Content, Help Articles, Forums, Blogs, and Wikis) to filter the results. You can use the Sort By links to view the results by categories such as relevance and rating.

After Office 365 displays search results, you can filter and sort them by selecting a category such as Forums and an option such as Most Recent.

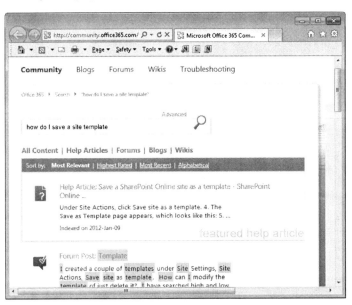

The Help button on the portal's home page opens the Office 365 Help page, which contains links to Help topics about specific applications and to information that gets you started with Office 365. (Unless you are responsible for administering an implementation of Office 365, you probably won't need to refer to the topics under Help For Admins.) The Help page also includes a search box you can use to locate information about a specific topic.

The Help page displays general categories you can browse through. Use the search box to find more detailed information.

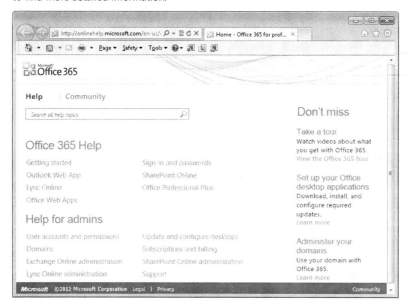

The following sections describe more about the Office 365 community forums and the other options for finding help and support.

Viewing Context-Sensitive Help

The Help content you want to see often depends on the task you are performing or the application you are working in. In Office 365, the Help content is tailored in this way. For example, when you switch to the Calendar view in Outlook (by clicking Calendar on the portal's home page, for example) and then click the Help button in Outlook, the topics that appear pertain to tasks such as sending a meeting request, using flags and reminders, and using the Scheduling Assistant to view your colleagues' free and busy times.

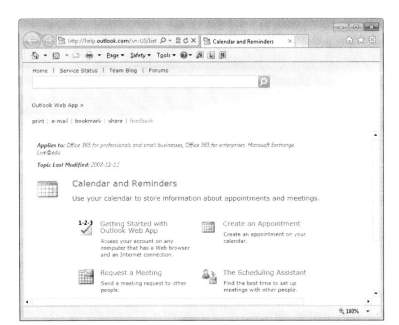

The Help topics displayed depend on the context you are working in.

Tip Use the links near the top of the page to print a Help topic; send a link to the topic in e-mail; bookmark the page; share it on sites such as Facebook, Twitter, or Windows Live; or offer feedback.

Using Office 365 Tutorials

Under the Start Here section on the portal's home page, you'll find links to animated overviews of Office 365 features and functionality and to a quick-start guide that reviews the essentials for working in Office 365. The guide explains features and provides the steps for basic procedures such as creating a contact in Outlook Web App and sending an instant message in Lync. (You'll learn how to perform these and many other detailed procedures in Chapters 2 through 4 as well.)

To find details for many tasks or to get an overview of Office 365, go to the portal's home page, click the Help button, and then click Getting Started under Office 365 Help. The Getting Started page is organized by category, with specific topics listed under headings such as Outlook and Lync.

When you are working in Outlook Web App, the Help page for each of the Outlook Web App views (Mail, Calendar, Contacts, and Tasks) has a link to an article named "Getting Started with Outlook Web App." Similarly, if you open the Help page for your SharePoint

Online, you can click the Getting Started link to see a list of topics that describe basic tasks and introduce the SharePoint ribbon, for example.

> **Tip** Among the Getting Started topics for your team site, you'll also find links to a series of articles that guide you through planning and managing a site collection. If you are responsible for implementing Office 365 or working with a group to plan your team site, these articles will prove helpful.

If you want an introduction to Lync, click Welcome To Lync on the Help menu in the Lync window to view an animated overview that also includes steps you can follow to make sure your phone and webcam work with Lync.

Reviewing Information in Community Forums

Using your Microsoft Online Services ID, you can create an account to participate in the Office 365 community, and thereby gain access to blogs and forums where you can learn more about specific topics and pose questions when you need help and advice from other Office 365 users and experts.

To set up a community account, click Participate In The Community, the last link under Community on the portal's home page. You simply need to enter the display name you want to use and click Join Now. The community site provides links to the latest postings on the blog (see the next section), recent forum discussions, technical Wikis, and other news of interest about who is using Office 365 and how they are using it.

Click Ask A Question In The Forums on the portal's home page to pose a question of your own or to search for information about a topic you are troubleshooting or exploring. (You can also click Forums near the top of the Community page or the blog.) Posts to the forums are organized in categories, with each forum category subdivided into topics. Under the topics, each discussion in a specific forum is listed. Click a column heading (Topic, Date, or Replies) to sort the discussions.

Forums are organized by service, and each main forum is divided into categories such as you see here for Lync.

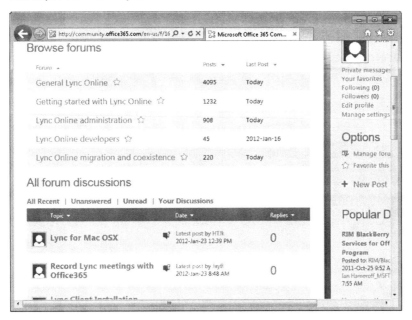

> **Tip** If you want to follow discussions on specific Office 365 forums, open the Forums page (click Ask A Question In The Forums on the portal home page) and then use links under Options (Manage Forum Subscriptions and Subscribe Via RSS) to set up the subscriptions you want.

Consulting Team Blogs

Click Check Out Our Blog in the group of community links on the home page to display the Office 365 Technical Blog. Like other support pages, the blog page provides a search box and sorting options.

Although some posts are more pertinent to the work of software developers and administrators than everyday users of Office 365, you can still find plenty of helpful information by scrolling through the list of blogs, sorting the list, or searching for information on a topic. Click Post A Question to the right of the search box to submit a question to readers of the Office 365 community forums.

Finding Technical Support

The Microsoft Support site provides a page dedicated to Office 365. The URL for the site is *support.microsoft.com/ph/15834*. This page contains a collection of links that are germane to standard users of Office 365 as well as to administrators. Select a category along the left side of the page to display links to articles about Office 365 applications, resolutions to common problems, and troubleshooting advice.

Go to the Office 365 support page on microsoft.com to view solutions to common issues, background information, and other resources.

> **Tip** You'll also find a link to support pages on *office365.com*. You can find information about deploying Office 365 and system requirements, links to the Office 365 blog and the Office 365 community site, and other information.

Using How-To Procedures and Solutions

As mentioned earlier, much of the Office 365 Help content is designed for specific contexts. The topics you discover by searching or by browsing the Help system often provide step-by-step procedures for performing specific tasks. For example, the following screen shot shows the Help topic for how to request a meeting. In addition to the how-to procedure shown for this task, you can use the links under Related Help Topics and Related Forum Or Blog Discussions.

Step-by-step procedures are provided for many common tasks.
Use the links on the right to find related information.

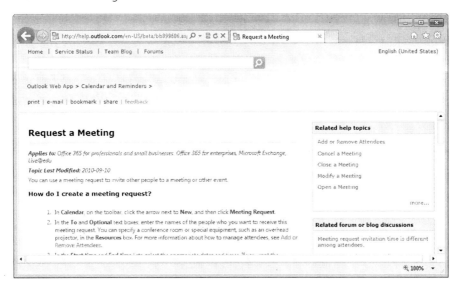

One other tool you can use to try and solve an issue is the Office 365 troubleshooting tool. To access this tool, start by clicking one of the community links on the portal's home page or go directly to *http://community.office365.com*. Then click the Troubleshooting heading near the top of the page.

The selections you make in the troubleshooting tool lead to a list of possible solutions to the problem you identify.

You work with the troubleshooting tool much like you work through one of the Office desktop wizards. Here, first select the plan and role that fits your situation, and then follow along by making selections that pertain to the issue you want to solve. For example, in step 2, select the service you are having trouble with, which might be SharePoint Online or Exchange Online (which you would choose if the problem is connected to Outlook Web App). With each selection you make, the troubleshooting tool progresses through its steps and displays a set of options that help you identify the particular problem you have. When you reach step 5, Possible Solutions, you'll see a list of topics that might include your particular issue. If you see a description that matches or closely resembles your issue, click the link to find more information. Otherwise, click Start Over to work through the troubleshooting tool again.

Practice Tasks

Practice the skills you learned in this section by performing the following tasks on your installation of Office 365:

- Sign in to Office 365.
- Use the links on the home page to open Outlook and your team site.
- Install Lync (if it is not already installed and you have permissions to install applications on your computer).
- View your profile, and add a picture if you want to.
- Sign up for the Office 365 community.
- Explore the Office 365 Help system, the blogs, and forum discussions.

1.2 Navigate Office 365 Applications

Two of the applications you'll use in Office 365 are Outlook Web App and SharePoint, which provides the foundation for your team site. In this section, you'll learn the basics of how to find your way around these applications. We'll look at Outlook first and then cover the SharePoint team site.

Using the Outlook Navigation Pane

The navigation pane appears along the left side of the Outlook Web App window. At the bottom of the navigation pane are links to your inbox, the calendar, the tasks list, and your list of contacts. To switch views, you need only to click the link for the view you want to work with. The navigation pane then shows items for that specific feature. For example, when you are looking at the Mail view, you'll see a list of favorite folders along with standards such as Inbox, Drafts, and Sent Items. At the top of the navigation pane for tasks and contacts, you'll see a set of options that let you filter the items that Outlook displays.

Use the navigation pane in Outlook Web App to organize and access items. Right-click an item in the navigation pane to display a menu with commands similar to what you see here for Calendar view.

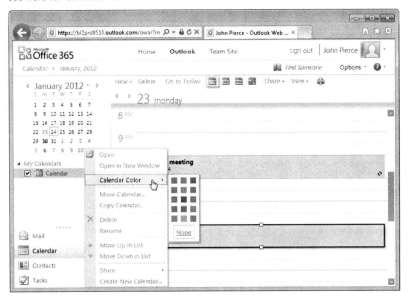

The following sections explain navigational features in each of the Outlook Web App views.

> **See Also** See Chapter 2 for details about working with e-mail, calendars, tasks, and contacts.

Navigating in Mail View

For e-mail, the navigation pane includes a set of default folders you will be familiar with if you use the desktop version of Outlook. Above the list of default folders is a set of favorites. The initial group of favorites are Inbox, Unread Mail, and Sent Items.

> **Tip** Click the arrow beside Favorites or the name of your account to collapse and expand the list of folders shown in the navigation pane.

To manage the Favorites list, you can use the Add To Favorites and Remove From Favorites commands. The relevant command appears on a menu that appears when you right-click a folder in the navigation pane. This menu also lets you work with e-mail folders and modify the view of the navigation pane in other ways. Use the menu to perform the following operations:

- Open a folder
- Open a folder in a new window
- Move or copy a folder
- Delete a folder
- Rename a folder
- Create a folder
- Mark items as read
- Empty the folder

You'll see a list of similar commands when you work in the Calendar, Contacts, or Tasks views.

➤ **To add a folder to the Favorites list**

→ In the navigation pane, right-click the folder you want to add, and then choose **Add to Favorites**.

➤ **To remove a folder from the Favorites list**

→ In the Favorites list, right-click the folder you want to delete from the list, and then choose **Remove from Favorites**.

➤ **To create a new folder in the navigation pane**

1. In the navigation pane, right-click your account name (or right-click a folder for which you want to create a subfolder).

2. From the menu, choose **Create New Folder**.

3. In the box that appears on the navigation pane, type a name for the folder.

Navigating in Calendar View

When you view the calendar, the navigation pane shows a thumbnail view of a monthly calendar at the top. You see the current month by default and can use the arrows at the right and left of the month's name to move ahead or back in time. You can also click the name of the month to pop up a menu that lets you choose an upcoming month or year or a month or year in the recent past.

Use the calendar control in the navigation pane to display an upcoming date or one in the recent past.

Under My Calendars, Outlook displays the default calendar and any other calendars you set up. Right-click My Calendars to display a menu that lets you rename, remove, or define a new calendar group. If you define at least one other calendar group (you can define more), the Move Up In List and Move Down In List commands become active on this menu. You can use these commands to change the order in which calendar groups are displayed in the navigation pane.

Right-clicking a specific calendar displays a menu with a number of other commands, including Open and Open In New Window and Move Up In List and Move Down In List. On this menu, the Move Up and Move Down commands apply to specific calendars, letting you reorder the calendars within a group. The Calendar Color command lets you assign the background color for a calendar.

> **See Also** You'll see how to work with other commands on this menu, including Share and Create New Calendar, in Chapter 2.

Navigating in Contacts View

In Contacts view, the navigation pane includes a set of filtering options in addition to a list of contact groups and folders. The filtering options are All, People, and Groups. These options let you see a specific list of contacts so that you can more easily locate and work with contacts you need.

By default, the contact folder list has a single group (My Contacts) that includes a folder named Contacts. Right-click My Contacts to display a menu with commands for renaming, removing, and creating groups; changing the order of contact groups in the list; and creating a new contacts folder.

> **Tip** If you create a contacts group of your own, these commands are also available when you right-click that group.

Right-click a contacts folder, and you gain access to commands like those you see for e-mail and calendars (and for tasks).

➤ **To filter the contacts list in the navigation pane**

1. Click **Contacts** at the bottom of the Outlook Web App window.

2. In the navigation pane's **Show** area, select the filtering option you want to apply: **All**, **People**, or **Groups**.

3. Double-click a contact item to display its details.

Navigating in Tasks View

As with contacts, the navigation pane in the Tasks view includes a set of filtering options above the list of task groups and task folders. The default configuration includes one task group, named My Tasks, and two task folders—Flagged Items And Tasks and Tasks. The Show options let you view all tasks (active and complete) or filter the view to see only active tasks, overdue tasks, or completed tasks.

As you can in other Outlook Web App views, you can right-click a task group or task folder to open a menu with commands that let you create groups and folders and change the order in which folders appear in the navigation pane.

➤ **To filter the task list in the navigation pane**

1. Click **Tasks** at the bottom of the Outlook Web App window.

2. In the navigation pane's **Show** area, select the filtering option you want to apply: **All**, **Active**, **Overdue**, or **Complete**.

3. Double-click a task item to display its details.

Navigating on Your Team Site

In Chapter 4, you'll learn the details of how to extend and add features to your team site. This section describes two basic navigational aids you'll use on the team site—the Quick Launch, which is displayed along the left side of the team site window, and the bread-crumb navigation, which you access by clicking the folder icon that appears next to Site Actions at the top of the window.

Use links in the Quick Launch at the left to open lists and libraries. Use the breadcrumbs, shown at the top, to navigate up to the home page or another location.

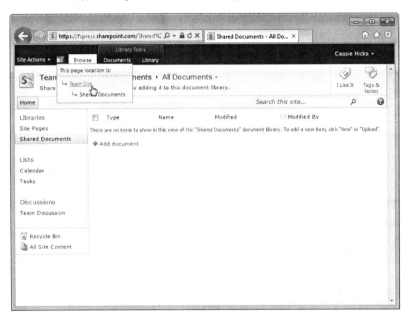

Using the Quick Launch

The links included on the Quick Launch let you display subsites, pages, lists, and libraries on your site with a single click. By default, links to the team site's pages, the Shared Documents library, the Calendar and Task lists, and the default Team Discussion appear on the Quick Launch. The Quick Launch also includes the links Recycle Bin and All Site Content.

You can retrieve pages or other items you delete from the Recycle Bin for up to 30 days. The All Site Content link takes you to a page that shows each element of your team site (lists and libraries, for example). You can open an item by clicking its link. If you have permission, you can click the Create link at the top of the page to initiate the steps you follow to add an element to your site.

When you click Site Pages on the Quick Launch, SharePoint displays a page from which you can edit the pages already on your site or add a page. In the list of current pages, move the pointer to the left end of a row, and SharePoint displays a check box. Select this check box to display commands on the ribbon. You use these commands to (among other operations) upload a document, edit properties, and configure settings for a list or library.

Clicking the Shared Documents link under Libraries leads you to a page you can use to upload a document to this library or create or edit a document already stored there.

When you build your team site by adding other lists and libraries, links to these items can be added to the Quick Launch to facilitate navigation.

Navigating Up with the Breadcrumbs

As you add elements to your default team site (such as lists, libraries, pages, and subsites), you can use the breadcrumbs tool to retrace your steps to a page higher in the site's hierarchy.

The breadcrumbs icon sits just to the right of the Site Actions menu. (The ScreenTip that you see when you point to this icon is Navigate Up.) When you click it, you'll see a simple depiction of the relationship of the page you are viewing to the site at large. To move up the site hierarchy—for example, to return to the team site home page—click the entry for the page you want to view.

➤ **To navigate using breadcrumbs**

1. Click the breadcrumbs icon.

2. Click the page you want to view.

Practice Tasks

Practice the skills you learned in this section by performing the following tasks on your installation of Office 365:

- Open your Outlook Web App inbox.

- Using the navigation pane, add folders for current projects, frequent e-mail correspondents, or other categories you use to organize your e-mail.

- Open the team site, and then open the Shared Documents library from the Quick Launch.

- Use the breadcrumbs to return to the team site's home page.

Objective Review

Before finishing this chapter, be sure you have mastered the following skills:

1.1 Navigate Office 365 features

1.2 Navigate Office 365 applications

2 Communicating by Using Office 365 Outlook Web App

The skills tested in this section of the Microsoft Office exam for Office 365 relate to using Outlook Web App. Each area of working with Outlook is covered. Specifically, the following objectives are associated with this set of skills:

2.1 Manage e-mail

2.2 Organize calendars

2.3 Manage contacts

2.4 Manage tasks

2.5 Configure Outlook Web App options

In Chapter 1, "Navigating Office 365," you learned about the Outlook Web App navigation pane and the application's main views. This chapter provides details about the work you do in each view, covering items such as creating inbox rules, using the Scheduling Assistant, importing contacts, and adding tasks. In this chapter's last main section, you'll learn about the various options you can set to manage your work in Outlook Web App.

2.1 Manage E-mail

This section describes how you work in Mail view—how you send and reply to e-mail messages, search for messages, work with file attachments, and define rules that Outlook applies to help you manage the flow of messages.

Creating and Sending Messages

You can create and send a simple e-mail message in a few steps:

1. Click **New** in the toolbar at the top of the Outlook Web App window, or press Ctrl+N.

> **Important** Your browser might block the message item from opening when you press Ctrl+N. Click Yes to display the pop-up window. If you use this keyboard combination often, consider changing the setting in your browser for how to handle pop-up windows.

2. In the message window, enter the e-mail addresses for recipients in the **To** and **Cc** lines, or click **To** or **Cc** to open the address book and select recipients.

3. Type a subject for the message and then the text of the message itself.

4. Click **Send**.

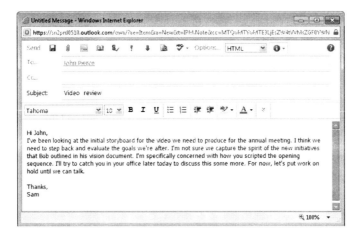

Use the toolbar at the top of a message window to add attachments and images and to check your spelling.

The formatting toolbar lets you emphasize text with effects such as different fonts, lists, and highlighting.

> **Tip** When you use the address book to select a message's recipients, select the name of the recipient, and then click To or Cc (or Bcc) at the bottom of the address book window. When you have selected all recipients, click OK to add them to the message.

For many messages, that's all you need to do, but Outlook Web App also provides tools for formatting and emphasizing information in the message, inserting images and file attachments, locating people you need to send the message to, checking spelling, and adding an e-mail signature.

You'll find these tools above the To line and below the Subject line. Use the toolbar above the To line to do the following:

- **Save**   Lets you save a draft of a message. Outlook displays the time a draft was saved in a notification bar above the To line.

- **Attach a file**   Click Attach File to include one or more file attachments with a message. Select the file or files in the Open dialog box, and then click Open. Outlook adds the Attachments field to the message and displays the names of the files.

> **See Also** You'll learn more details in "Working with Attachments" later in this chapter.

- **Insert a picture**   You can use the Attach File button to include an image file as an attachment, but click Insert Picture when you want to place an image in the body of the message itself. After you select the image and click Open in the Open dialog box, Outlook loads the picture, initially showing the file name and size in the Attached field and indicating that the image is inline. You might also see an icon for the image in the message body as Outlook works to insert the image. When the picture is in place, Outlook Web App displays a ScreenTip that reads Click To Resize when you point to the image. Click the image to display a menu with various options for resizing the picture—Small, Medium, Original, Large, and Fit To Window.

- **Open your address book**   Use your address book to initiate a message to one of your contacts or contact groups. Right-click on the contact, and then choose New Message.

- **Check names**   Verifies whether e-mail addresses are complete and also confirms whether an address matches an entry in your address book. If Outlook can't resolve an address, it displays the notification No Match Was Found and provides a link you can use to remove the address.

- **Set importance**   Specify high importance for a message when you want recipients to attend to its content as soon as possible. Use the low importance option to indicate that a message doesn't include critical information or need anyone's attention right away.

- **Insert your signature**   Adds a signature you've defined to the message. (You can't add a signature until you define one. For more information, see "Mail Settings" later in this chapter.)

- **Check spelling**   Run the spelling checker by clicking this button. Outlook Web App identifies with squiggly underlining any words that might be misspelled. Right-click an underlined word to see a list of suggestions you can choose from or click Ignore or Ignore All. If Outlook finds no spelling errors, it displays a message in the notification bar at the top of the message window. Use the arrow to the right of the Check Spelling button to open a menu from which you can choose a different language to check for spelling errors.

- **Set message options**   The Options button opens a dialog box in which you can set message importance, choose to display the Bcc or From field, and specify a tracking option that lets you know when the message has been delivered and read. (You can select both tracking options.) The message at the bottom of this dialog box directs you to open the main Outlook Web App Options page to set additional options.

> **See Also** You'll learn more about working on the Options page in "Configure Outlook Web App Options" later in this chapter.

- **Specify a message format**   You can send messages in HTML format or as plain text. If you choose Plain Text from this list, Outlook Web App hides the formatting toolbar. Any text in the message uses a default font. Keep in mind that some recipients of e-mail might prefer plain text messages that don't include extensive formatting. In addition, the e-mail programs that some recipients use might not have the capability to render messages formatted with HTML. Outlook Web App converts any images inserted in a message to attachments if you switch from HTML to plain text.

- **Display the notification bar**   Click the information icon to show or hide the notification bar. Notifications are shown by default.

With the formatting toolbar (which appears below the Subject line), you can choose a different font for all or a portion of the message's text, select a font size, add character formatting (bold, underline, and italic), set up numbered or bulleted lists, highlight text, and so on.

Click the down arrow at the right of the formatting toolbar to open a menu you can use to add other formatting tools. Among the options included are those for inserting a hyperlink or a horizontal rule or aligning text to the left, center, or right. Select the check box for a tool you want to add or remove from the toolbar. Outlook Web App retains the changes you make to this toolbar so that they are available when you initiate another new message or open Outlook Web App again.

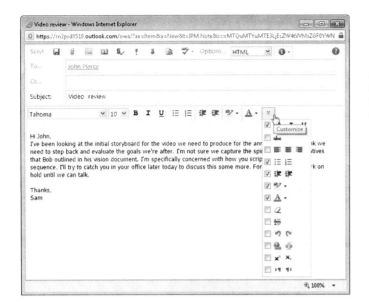

Select items on the Customize menu to update the formatting toolbar with effects you frequently use.

➤ To create and send an e-mail message

1. Click **New** in the toolbar at the top of the Outlook Web App window (or press Ctrl+N).

2. In the message window, enter the e-mail addresses for recipients in the **To** and **Cc** lines.

3. Type a subject for the message and then the text of the message itself.

4. Use the toolbar to insert attachments or images, set importance, add a signature, set message options, and choose a message format (HTML or plain text).

5. If you use the HTML message format, apply formatting using the toolbar below the **Subject** line.

6. Click **Send**.

Reviewing and Replying to Messages

By default, Outlook provides two views of your e-mail messages. To the right of the navigation pane, messages are displayed in a list. To the right of the message list, the message selected in the message list is shown in the reading pane. In the next two sections, you'll learn how you can review messages in each view and about your options for replying to a message.

By default, Mail view shows messages in a list, organized by conversation, and with the selected message displayed in the reading pane.

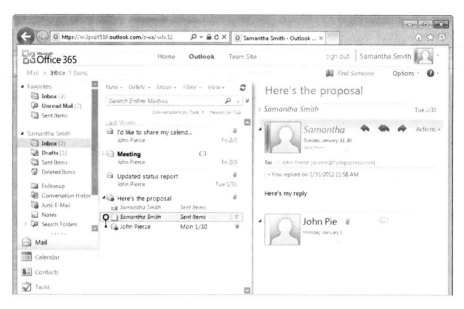

> **Tip** Use the View menu on the toolbar to display the reading pane at the bottom of the window or to display it again at the right side of the window (its default position).

Reviewing Conversations

Outlook Web App organizes messages into conversations, which means that messages with a common subject line that you and others send and receive are grouped as a single item in the message list and shown together in the reading pane. As you can see in the preceding screen shot, items in a conversation are identified by sender, and Outlook also indicates which folder an item is stored in and other message details. Items not stored in the inbox are shown in italic.

You can manage your view of conversations and the items a conversation contains in several ways:

- Use the arrow beside a message header in the message list to show or hide the conversation tree.

- Use the arrow beside a message in the reading pane to display or hide details for an item.

- In the message list, select or clear the check box beside an item in the conversation tree to show or hide details about this message in the reading pane. (The check box appears when you point to the left of the message.)

- Double-click an item in the message list or the reading pane to open it in its own window.

- Right-click an item in the message list (or open the Actions menu in the reading pane), and choose Ignore Conversation. When you choose this command, Outlook deletes messages that are part of this conversation (except for those in the Sent Items folder) and will also delete messages sent to that conversation in the future.

To turn off this feature, click Use Conversations on the View menu so that you clear the check mark. The Use Conversations command can be enabled for one folder and turned off for another. For example, you can view conversations in your inbox but not in the Deleted Items folder.

> **See Also** You'll learn about options for how you can organize conversations in "Mail Options" later in this chapter.

Sorting Messages

When you are reviewing messages in any folder, two links below the search box provide options for how the list of messages is sorted. To help you find a message you need to review, you can sort by date, by sender, by size, and by other criteria. If you choose Type, for example, items are sorted into categories such Message and Meeting Request. Clear the Conversation check box if you want to turn off conversations while tracking down a message.

Messages are sorted by date received by default. Use this menu to choose a different category.

If Use Conversations is enabled, the link on the left indicates how conversations are ordered (Conversations By Date, for example, or Conversations By From). If Use Conversations is turned off, the link reads Arrange By, but the menu of sorting options is the same.

The link at the right lets you change the order of the message list. The default order is Newest On Top. Click this link to change the order to Oldest On Top.

Replying to Messages

In reply to some e-mail messages, you can delete the message or file it away in an applicable folder. For messages that require further action on your part, you will take one of the following steps:

- Reply to the message's sender.
- Reply to all recipients of the message.
- Forward the message to someone not included on the original message.

You can perform these actions in a number of ways:

- In the reading pane, click the Reply, Reply All, or Forward button, options which are represented by the thick arrows beside the sender's name.
- In the reading pane, open the Actions menu, and then choose Reply, Reply All, or Forward.

> **Tip** Choose Forward As Attachment to include the message as an attachment to a new message.

- In the message list, right-click an item and choose Reply, Reply All, or Forward.
- Double-click an item in the message list or the reading pane to open the item in a separate window. On the toolbar, click Reply, Reply All, or Forward.

The window that Outlook displays when you reply to or forward a message contains the same fields and toolbar options as a new message window. In replies, the To line is filled in with the name of the sender or with all recipients of the message (including those originally in the Cc line) depending on the command you choose. When you forward a message, you need to fill in the addresses for recipients.

➤ **To review messages**

1. Use the **View** menu on the toolbar to display the reading pane at the right or bottom of the Outlook Web App window.

2. In the message list, select the message you want to review. Outlook displays the message in the reading pane.

3. To open a message in a separate window, double-click the message in the message list.

➤ **To work with conversations**

1. If conversations are not enabled for a folder, click **Use Conversations** on the **View** menu.

2. In the message list, click the arrow beside an item to expand the conversation tree.

3. In the reading pane, click the arrow beside an item to see the item details.

4. To delete the items in a conversation, right-click an item in the message list and choose **Ignore Conversation**.

➤ **To reply to or forward a message**

1. In the message list, right-click the message and choose **Reply**, **Reply All**, or **Forward**.

2. Type your reply or forwarding message, add formatting and attachments (if necessary), and then click **Send**.

Working with Other E-mail Commands

In addition to Reply, Reply All, and Forward, the Actions menu and the menu that appears when you right-click a message include commands that let you mark a message as unread, create a rule based on properties of the message (you'll learn more about rules later in this section), move and copy the message item, and perform other operations.

Searching and Filtering Your Message Store

To locate messages in Outlook Web App, you can filter the message list and use the search box.

Filtering Messages

Choose an option on the Filter menu, shown in the following screen shot, to show only messages sent to you, messages on which you are copied (included on the Cc line), messages with attachments, or messages sent with high importance, among other settings. For the Category and From commands, choose an option from the submenu to specify the detailed filter. Click Apply to display the results of the filter you select.

Apply a filter to view a subset of your messages— such as all those with high importance or all those from a specific sender.

Filters apply to the current folder. In other words, if you filter your inbox to show only messages you are copied on, the Sent Items folder or another e-mail folder isn't automatically filtered by that criterion as well. You need to apply this filter again to achieve the same view.

When you apply a filter, Outlook displays a notification bar beneath the search box. The notification indicates which folder you are working in and which filter you applied. At the far right of this notification bar, Outlook displays two additional toolbar buttons. Click Add Filter To Favorites if you want to save this view of the folder and have access to it from the navigation bar. Click Clear Filter to return to the unfiltered view of the items in the current folder.

You can add a filtered view you want to see frequently to the Favorites list.

Searching Messages

With a basic search operation, you can locate messages throughout your mailbox (all folders) that match the criteria you enter in the search box. The results include those items with matching text in the message body and subject line and in the names of persons that messages are from.

To change the search scope, click the down arrow to the right of the search button and then choose This Folder, This Folder And Subfolders, or Entire Mailbox. Change the default location (which is initially set to Entire Mailbox) if you want to narrow the search scope to the current folder or the current folder and its subfolders.

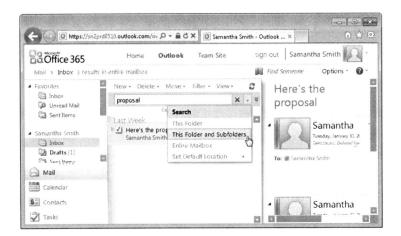

Change the search scope to look for messages in a specific folder or a folder and its subfolders.

You can expand search options by clicking the double down arrow beside the search box. Select the check box next to the search option you want to use. In the Results In list, specify whether to search the message body and subject line or just one or the other. The middle option lets you limit the search only to messages from or to the person you specify. You can also search by category.

> **See Also** For more information about using categories, see "Using Categories, Flags, and Reminders" later in this chapter.

To clear the current search term to restore the full message list, click the delete button (the red X) at the right end of the search box.

➤ To filter messages

1. From the **Filter** menu, choose the criteria you want to apply.

2. Click **Apply**.

3. Click **Clear Filter** to display the full message list again.

➤ To search messages

1. In the search box, type the term or phrase to search for.

2. Click the search button, or press Enter.

3. Click the delete button to display the full message list again.

➤ **To change the search scope**

1. Click the down arrow beside the search box.

2. Set the search scope: **This Folder**, **This Folder and Subfolders**, or **Entire Mailbox**.

3. Choose **Set Default Location**, and choose a location if you want to change the default search scope.

➤ **To work with advanced search options**

1. Click the double down arrow beside the search box.

2. Select the check box for the search options you want to use:

   ○ In the Results In list, select **Message body**, **Subject**, or **Subject and message body**.

   ○ Specify whether you want to search messages from or sent to an individual, and then enter the name or e-mail address in the text box.

   ○ Choose a category.

3. In the search box, type the term or phrase to search for.

4. Click the search button, or press Enter.

5. Click the delete button (the red X) to clear the search box and display the full message list again.

Working with Attachments

To add an attachment to a message, click Attach File (the paper clip icon) in the message item's toolbar. In the Open dialog box, select the file or files you want to attach and click Open, and then the files are added to the message item. To delete an attachment before you send a message, click the delete button beside the file name.

When you are reading e-mail, you can work with attachments in the reading pane or in the message item. In the reading pane, if you don't see attachment file names, click the paper clip icon to reveal them. Then, click Open In Browser (to the right of the attachment) to view the file in your browser. (For most Office files, you will view the file in the associated program's web app.) Double-click the file name when you want to open the file in its native application or save the file. If you are working in Internet Explorer 9, you'll see the notification bar at the bottom of the Outlook Web App window. Click

Open, or use one of the options available with the Save button. Click Save to place the file in the default folder for downloads. Click Save As to choose a different location in which to save the file, or click Save And Open to save the file to the default location and then open it.

> **Tip** In browsers other than Internet Explorer, the processes for opening and saving an attachment are slightly different. For example, in Firefox 10.0, you see a dialog box with the options Open With and Save File.

You can perform the same operations by double-clicking an item in the message list to open it and then working with the file attachments.

➤ **To add an attachment**

1. On the message window's toolbar, click **Attach File**.

2. In the **Open** dialog box, select the file or files you want to attach and then click **Open**.

➤ **To view an attachment in your browser**

➜ In the **Attachments** field, click **Open in Browser**.

➤ **To open or save an attachment**

1. Double-click the attached file.

2. Follow the directions provided by your browser to open or save your file.

Using Inbox Rules

By combining actions, criteria, and exceptions to define an inbox rule, you gain a high degree of control over where and how Outlook routes and handles your messages. For example, you can create a rule that routes messages from specific users to a folder you designate. You can also apply rules to route messages on the basis of text in a message's subject line.

Creating a Rule

To define an inbox rule, you work on the Outlook Options page. Click Options in the top-right corner of the Outlook window and choose Create An Inbox Rule.

The first element of a rule is the action you want to use as the basis of the rule. You can choose from five starting points, as shown here:

Start by selecting a basic rule that you build on to manage the flow of specific messages.

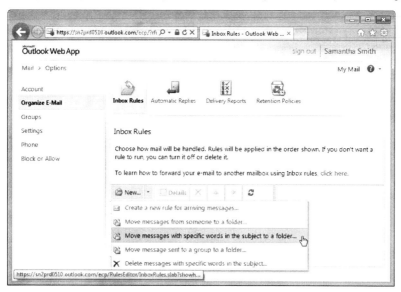

The choices shown on the New menu lead to a dialog box that prompts you to fill in certain information—for example, specific words in the subject line you want Outlook to act on. But the option you choose from this menu doesn't exclude other possibilities. You have access to all actions and criteria when you start a rule—you just get a head start by choosing an option here.

> **Tip** The default option that Outlook displays if you simply click New, is Create A New Rule For Arriving Messages.

In general, the steps you follow and the type of information you enter and specify are the same for each type of rule. For example, if you select the option Move Messages

With Specific Words In The Subject To A Folder, Outlook sets up the New Inbox Rule dialog box as shown here:

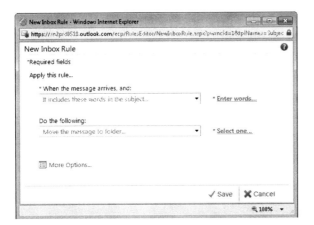

You refine a rule by defining conditions and actions. Click More Options to add additional criteria and to define exceptions to the rule.

Click Enter Words, and then type the words or phrase you want Outlook to act on. In the Specify Words Or Phrases dialog box, be sure to click the plus sign after you add each word or phrase to the rule. Click OK after you add the terms.

Click Select One, and then choose the folder you want messages routed to. You might use this rule to manage messages related to specific projects, for example. As long as project team members include the project name or another identifying phrase in the subject of the message, Outlook applies this rule.

In many instances, straightforward rules defined with a single condition and action are all you need. To build more complex rules, click More Options in the New Inbox Rule dialog box. With these additional options available, you can add conditions or actions to rules, define exceptions, choose to stop rule processing when Outlook applies this rule, and name the rule. In the following screen shot, the rule is defined to move messages with "Status Report" in the subject line to the folder named Followup and also to assign these messages to the Blue category. These steps will be followed except when such a message is marked with high importance.

This rule applies two actions to messages that meet the defined condition and also includes an exception for messages with high importance.

Basing a Rule on a Message

You can create a rule based on the details of a message by right-clicking the message in the message list and choosing Create Rule. In the New Inbox Rule dialog box, the action specified is When The Message Arrives, And. The sender and recipient names are already included, and the text of the subject line is set up as a condition you can apply to the rule. Choose options to complete the action, specify what you want Outlook to do (such as moving the message to a folder), and click More Options if you want to create additional actions, conditions, and exceptions.

Managing Rules

More than one rule can apply to a message. For example, you might set up a rule to route messages from Samantha Smith to one folder and a rule that routes messages with "Status Report" in the subject line to a different folder. If Samantha sends you a message about a status report, which rule applies? Rules are processed in the order in which they appear in the list of rules shown on the Options page. On this page, you can change the order of rules by selecting a rule and using the Move Up and Move Down buttons. To turn off a rule, clear the check box in the On column. To view the details of a rule or to make changes to a rule, select the rule and then click Details to open the Edit Rule dialog box, where you change or define actions, conditions, and exceptions.

Inbox rules are processed in the order they are listed. Move a message up or down to change that sequence.

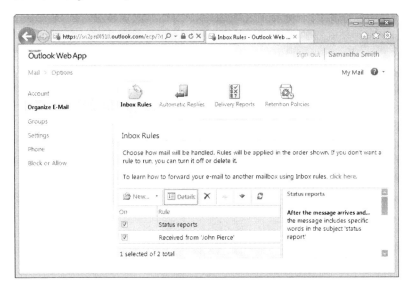

➤ To create an inbox rule

1. At the top-right corner of the Outlook window, click **Options**, **Create an Inbox Rule**.

2. On the **Options** page, under **Inbox Rules**, click the arrow next to **New**, and then select the basic rule you want to use.

3. In the **New Inbox Rule** dialog box, under **Apply this rule**, select the condition you want to apply to the rule.

4. Under **Do the following**, select the action you want Outlook to take when the rule's conditions are met.

5. To add conditions, actions, and exceptions, click **More Options**, and then use the **Add** buttons to define additional elements of the rule.

6. Select **Stop processing more rules** if you don't want Outlook to apply other rules to messages that meet the conditions of the rule you are defining.

7. Type a name for the rule, and then click **Save**.

➤ To manage rules

1. At the top-right corner of the Outlook window, click **Options**, **Create an Inbox Rule**.

2. In the list of rules, select the rule you want to work with.

3. To reposition the rule (so that the order in which rules are processed is altered), use the **Move Up** or **Move Down** button.

4. Click **Details** to open the **Inbox Rule** dialog box and make changes to the definition of the rule.

5. Click the **Delete** button to remove a rule.

6. Clear the check box in the **On** column for a rule to deactivate the rule.

Practice Tasks

Practice the skills you learned in this section by performing the following tasks in Outlook Web App:

- Create and send several e-mail messages to become familiar with the Outlook Web App user interface.

- Reposition the reading pane, and turn it off to see different views of the Outlook window.

- Work with colleagues or coworkers to create a conversation. Use the message list and the reading pane to expand the conversation tree and see the message details Outlook provides.

- Search for messages using the sender's last name.

- Create an inbox rule that moves messages from one of your friends or coworkers to a folder you create.

2.2 Organize Calendars

Keeping track of your appointments and meeting schedule is the main operation you perform in Calendar view. Outlook Web App provides a number of tools you use to add items to your calendar and a variety of features you use to manage them, including several ways to share your calendar with others. You'll learn about these areas of Outlook in the following sections.

Recording Appointments

To enter a new appointment, first display the day of the appointment in Day view, Work Week view, or Week view. Point to the time when the appointment occurs, and then double-click the calendar to open a new appointment item. You can also choose Appointment from the New menu to open an appointment item.

> **Tip** To quickly schedule an all-day event, switch the calendar to Month view and then double-click the date for the event.

> **See Also** To learn more about calendar views, see "Switching Calendar Views" later in this chapter.

An appointment item contains fields such as Start Time, End Time, and Location. Fill in these fields with the details of the appointment, and make changes to the default reminder (which is set to display a notification for 15 minutes before the scheduled start time). Clear the Reminder check box to do without a reminder.

The Show Time As list provides four options—Busy, Away, Free, and Tentative. Use Busy to mark confirmed appointments. Use Away to designate time spent away from work on a vacation or a business trip. Because other users can view your free/busy information, mark unconfirmed appointments as Tentative.

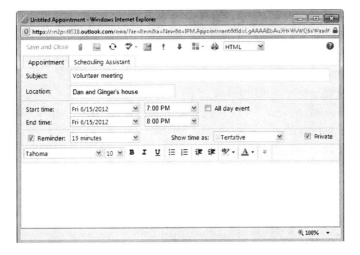

An appointment item includes a subject and the time and place. Reset the reminder if you want Outlook to notify you further ahead than 15 minutes.

Many of the controls on the appointment item toolbar provide the same functionality as for e-mail messages. You can check spelling, add attachments, apply formats, mark importance, and so on. You can apply formatting only to the text you add to the notes section of an appointment item.

> **See Also** For details about commands on the appointment item toolbar, see "Creating and Sending Messages" earlier in this chapter.

> ➤ **To set up an appointment**

1. In Calendar view, click **New**, **Appointment** on the toolbar.

2. Fill in the appointment item with the start and end times.

3. Make adjustments to the reminder if necessary.

4. Click **Save and Close**.

Working with Meeting Requests

Meeting arrangements, such as time and place and who needs to attend, are facilitated by using meeting requests. In this section, you'll learn how to set up and send a meeting request and about the options you have when you reply to one.

> **See Also** For information about options for how Outlook Web App can automatically process meeting requests you receive, see "Calendar Settings" later in this chapter.

Sending a Meeting Request

In the form you use to set up a meeting request, use the To line to list required invitees. Type e-mail addresses or contact names, or click To and then select invitees from the address book. (Click Check Names on the toolbar to verify names you enter yourself.) Use the Optional line to add the addresses of people whom you want to make aware of the meeting but whose attendance isn't required. In the Resources field, you can select conference rooms or pieces of equipment that are listed in the shared address book. Also include the subject of the meeting, and use the Location line to indicate where the meeting will be held (if this information isn't specified under Resources).

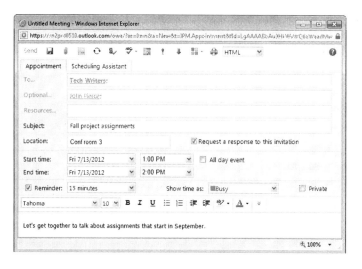

You receive responses by default when you send a meeting request. You can invite coworkers as well as resources such as conference rooms that are listed in your address book.

> **See Also** You'll learn more about an important component you can use with meeting requests—the Scheduling Assistant—later in this section.

Other details you need to specify are the meeting's start and end times and how you want your calendar to display the scheduled time slot. By default, the time slot is marked as Busy, but you can choose Tentative for a time that's not confirmed. (You can also set the Show Time As setting to Free or Away if either of these options apply.)

Select All Day Event if you are scheduling a day-long, offsite planning meeting, for example. Select Private if you don't want the other people viewing your calendar to see the details of this meeting. You can also adjust the timing of the reminder.

Before sending the meeting request, you can add information about the meeting in the body of the form. Use the toolbar to add attachments (perhaps a meeting agenda), set importance, or specify a category for the meeting. If you are using the HTML message format, you can use the formatting toolbar to change fonts, emphasize text with bold, set up a numbered or bulleted list, and so on.

By default, a meeting organizer receives replies from those invited to a meeting, indicating whether someone plans to attend or not. If you don't want to receive these replies, clear the check box for Request A Response To This Invitation.

> **See Also** If you are setting up a meeting that will occur regularly, click the Repeat button on the item toolbar to open the Repetition dialog box. For detailed information about setting up recurring items, see "Setting Up Repeating Tasks" later in this chapter.

Responding to a Meeting Request

Meeting requests that others send to you arrive in your inbox. In reply, you can accept the meeting, accept tentatively, or decline the request. The controls you use to respond to the request appear next to the meeting time.

Click the check mark to accept a meeting request, the question mark to say maybe, or the X if you can't attend.

By default, meeting requests you receive are added to your calendar and the time slot is shown as Tentative. (You can clear this setting in the Options dialog box. For details, see "Calendar Settings" later in this chapter.) No matter which option you select—Accept, Tentative, or Decline—you can edit your response (for example, you might want to explain why you need to decline a meeting), send your response without further comments, or not send a response. You can also use the Reply, Reply All, or Forward buttons in the meeting request's toolbar to correspond with the sender or with others about the meeting.

➤ To send a meeting request

1. In Calendar view, click **New**, **Meeting Request**.
2. Use the **To**, **Optional**, and **Resources** lines to add attendees and resources (such as conference rooms) from the address book. You can also type addresses in these fields.
3. Type the subject and location.
4. Specify the start and end times, and make any changes to the default reminder.
5. Add attachments and notes to the meeting request, and then click **Send**.

➤ To respond to a meeting request

1. Open the request.
2. Use the controls next to the meeting details to accept, accept tentatively, or decline the request.

Using the Scheduling Assistant

The Scheduling Assistant provides a view of when people in your organization who you want to include in a meeting (and rooms you can use to assemble) are free or busy. (You can't see free and busy information for external contacts.)

Click the Scheduling Assistant tab on the meeting request form. If you already included attendees or resources on the To, Optional, or Resource lines, those names are listed under Select Attendees in the Scheduling Assistant. You can remove any entries from this list or click Add A Name to include others on the meeting request.

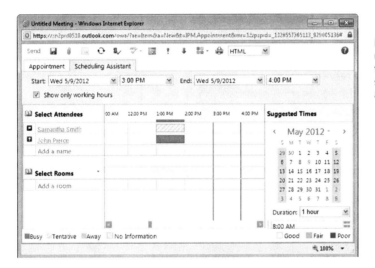

In the Scheduling Assistant, use the Start and End fields, the time scale, or one of the suggested times to set up a meeting.

Use the Start and End lists to set or adjust the date and time of the meeting. You can also click on the time scale to select a date and time or click a date on the thumbnail calendar to display a different date. Use the Duration list to specify a time different from the default one hour.

The time scale shows when the people and rooms selected are busy and free. The list at the bottom right of the window shows you blocks of open time and how many of the invitees are available then. (The legends at the bottom of the window indicate how Outlook displays free and busy times.)

When you finish setting up the Scheduling Assistant, switch back to the Appointment tab and add information about the meeting as necessary. When you are ready, click Send.

➤ **To work with the Scheduling Assistant**

1. In Calendar view, click **New, Meeting Request** on the toolbar.
2. Click the **Scheduling Assistant** tab.

3. Click **Select Attendees**, and then use the address book to add people and resources to the **To**, **Optional**, and **Resources** lines. Click **OK** in the address book.

4. On the time scale, select a time when meeting participants are free. You can also use the **Start** and **End** lists to specify the time for the meeting, select a date from the calendar, or select one of the free times proposed by the Scheduling Assistant.

5. Adjust the meeting duration if necessary.

6. Click the **Appointment** tab.

7. Add any message or attachments you want to include with the meeting request, and then click **Send**.

Setting Up Shared Calendars and Managing Permissions

You don't need to record all your appointments and meetings on a single calendar. For example, you might create a calendar to use for a specific project or to keep track of appointments related to family time or volunteer work. You can share your default calendar (named Calendar in Outlook) or calendars you create so that other people can see when you are free and busy.

> **Tip** To create a calendar, right-click My Calendars in the navigation pane and choose Create New Calendar. Then simply type the name for the calendar in the text box Outlook Web App displays.

Sharing a Calendar

Sharing a calendar takes only a few steps. In Calendar view, select the calendar you want to share. Open the Share menu, choose Share This Calendar, address the invitation, set sharing options, type a message if you need to, and then click Send.

The main step to consider is selecting the sharing option you want to provide to the person or persons you've addressed the message to. These options depend on whether you are sharing your default calendar (which is named Calendar). For your default calendar, Outlook gives you the following choices:

- Share only free and busy information. People with whom you share your calendar won't see any details about specific appointments or meetings.

- In addition to free and busy information, share information about the subject and location of meetings and appointments (the information included in those fields).

- Share all information, such as attachments that might be part of a meeting request or comments added to the body of an appointment or meeting item.

> **Tip** You can make sharing your calendar a reciprocal act by selecting the check box I Want To Request Permission To View The Recipient's Calendar Folder.

If you share a calendar you created, you can share all information or share all information and give people within your organization permission to add, edit, and delete information. By choosing this option, you can essentially create a group calendar that a team can use to schedule work for a project or an event.

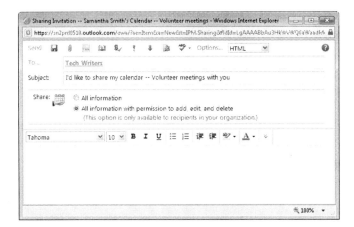

If you share a calendar with a group, choose the option to let members add, edit, and delete information to let all members update scheduled events.

Invitations to share a calendar are sent to the recipient's inbox. Open the invitation and then click the Add This Calendar link to start viewing the shared calendar. Outlook creates a group on the navigation bar named People's Calendars and lists the shared calendar there. Select the check box to display the calendar.

Changing Sharing Permissions

If you want to change which information a person you've shared your calendar with can see, choose the Change Sharing Permissions command from the Share menu to open the Calendar Permissions dialog box. (The name of the calendar you are working with appears in a heading at the top of the dialog box.) If you no longer want to share your calendar with someone, select the entry for that person and click Delete (the black X). Click Edit if you want to change sharing permissions. You can select one of the other options initially provided.

> **➤ To share your calendar**

1. On the **Share** menu, select **Share This Calendar**.

2. Address the sharing invitation to the people you want to share the calendar with.

3. Specify what information you want to share. The options available depend on the calendar you are sharing.

4. Add a message about the calendar (if necessary).

5. Click **Send**.

➤ To change calendar permissions

1. On the **Share** menu, select **Change Sharing Permissions**.

2. In the **Calendar** dialog box, under **Shared With**, select the person whose permissions you want to change.

3. To update this person's permissions, click **Edit**, and then set the permission level you want to grant.

4. Click **Delete** (the black X) to stop sharing the calendar with this person.

5. Click the **Refresh** button to update the information displayed in the dialog box.

Publishing Calendars

One or more of your calendars might contain information you want others to see. By publishing a calendar to the Internet, you let friends, family, colleagues in volunteer groups, and others outside your organization see when you are free or busy. You can also control the level of detail people viewing your calendar can see, the time span the calendar displays, and who has access to the calendar.

On the toolbar, choose Publish This Calendar To Internet from the Share menu to open the Calendar Publishing dialog box.

For a shared calendar, you specify the level of detail others can see, the time span shown, and the access level.

The options in the Publishing Detail list control whether people can see only your free and busy times (Availability Only), limited details, or full details. The Limited Details setting allows people to see the subject of meetings but not full details, such as location. Full Details provides all the details recorded about a meeting or an appointment.

Use the settings under Publish My Calendar to specify the time span shown in the calendar. You can choose settings between one day and one year. (You cannot enter your own values for these settings.) Choose one day before and after today to expose your calendar for a short duration, which could be helpful if someone you don't work with regularly is trying to schedule in the next few days a group meeting that involves you. Settings for access level let you restrict the calendar to only those people you provide a link to or open the calendar to the public, which means people can search for your calendar and locate it online.

Click Start Publishing when you finish setting options. Outlook then displays URLs for the calendar under Calendar Links. Use the link provided to copy these links to the Clipboard. People can use the first link to subscribe to this calendar, which means they are notified when the calendar is updated. Use the second link to let people view the calendar in their browser.

> **Tip** After you publish a calendar to the Internet, you'll find the Send Links To This Calendar command on the Share menu. Choose that command to create an e-mail invitation to share the calendar. The invitation includes the links for subscribing to the calendar and viewing it.

To make adjustments for a calendar you published, click Share, Change Publishing Settings. You can change the settings for the details you publish, the time span shown, and the access level. Click Stop Publishing if you no longer want to share this calendar on the Internet.

➤ To publish a calendar

1. Display and select the calendar you want to publish.
2. On the **Share** menu, select **Publish This Calendar to Internet**.
3. In the **Calendar Publishing** dialog box, select the level of detail to provide, the time span for sharing, and the access level.
4. Click **Start Publishing**.

➤ To change publishing settings

1. Display and select the calendar you published.
2. On the **Share** menu, select **Change Publishing Settings**.

3. Make changes to the level of detail, time span, and access level.

4. Send the links provided to people who want to subscribe to or view the calendar.

Adding Calendars

You can view calendars of people in your organization and calendars that have been published to the Internet. In the dialog box Outlook opens when you choose Add Calendar from the Share menu, select the option for the type of calendar you want to add and then specify the name of the person in your organization (you can add only one name to this box) or the URL for a calendar on the Internet.

For people in your organization, calendars are added to the People's Calendars group. (Outlook creates this group if it is not already present.) Calendars from the Internet are added to the Other Calendars group.

➤ To add a calendar

1. On the **Share** menu, select **Add Calendar**.

2. In the Add **Calendar** dialog box, choose the option to add a calendar from your organization or from the Internet.

3. Specify the name of the person in your organization or the URL for a calendar on the Internet.

4. Click **OK**.

Using Categories, Flags, and Reminders

How you work with categories, flags, and reminders applies not only to calendar items but to other types of Outlook items as well. For example, you can also assign e-mail messages, tasks, and contacts to categories; you can set up reminders for tasks; and you can set follow-up flags for e-mail, tasks, and contact items. Parts of this section focus on calendar items, but you can apply what you learn to other item types as well.

Assigning Items to Categories

You can assign any item to a category. This step helps organize items, of course, but it also provides a marker by which you can locate some items among many, because you can search by category when you are looking for mail messages, contacts, or tasks.

Outlook provides six color-coded categories. You can apply one or more of these built-in categories to items, but Outlook also lets you define your own categories—and you can use names that are more specific than Red, Blue, Yellow, and so on. You might, for example, create a category for each of your work projects, for individuals in a group you manage, or for the set of events you're currently planning.

To assign an item to a category, open the item and then click the Apply Categories button on the toolbar. Select the check boxes for the categories you want to associate this item with.

> **Tip** For tasks, the Apply Categories menu also appears on the toolbar above the task list, so you don't need to open the task item to assign it to a category. Simply select a task in the list, click Apply Categories, and then apply the categories you want.

To update and define categories, click Manage Categories on the menu. In the Manage Categories dialog box, do the following:

- Select a category and then click Delete Category to remove it. You need to confirm this action, and be sure to note that deleting the category does not affect any items assigned to it, except that the category is removed from the items.

- Select a category and then click Change Category Color if you want to update the color coding for a category. You cannot rename a category using this command, and you will likely apply it to a category you define rather than to the built-in categories.

- Click Create New Category to open a dialog box in which you name the category you want to create and associate it with a color (or no color). Categories you create are available to items in any view, but they are not available automatically to other people in your organization.

Flagging Items

Flags are a feature you can use to mark e-mail, task, and contact items for follow-up. For example, you can add a flag to a contact item to indicate the date when you need to write or call the contact again. You can flag an e-mail item for follow-up next week if you don't have the information required to reply to it today.

Flags can be set for different durations. The built-in choices are Today, Tomorrow, This Week, Next Week, and No Date. Today is the default value, but you can change this setting. You can also set a flag for a specific date (by typing the date or choosing it from a calendar control) and set a start date, due date, and reminder for the work requiring follow-up.

To add the default flag to an e-mail message or task, select the item in the list of items in that view and then click the blank flag. To add a flag with a different duration (and to manage flags in general), right-click the flag icon for the item and then choose the flag you want.

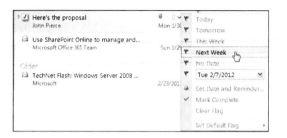

Keep track of assignments, replies, and calls you need to make to contacts by flagging items in Outlook.

> **Tip** For contact items, add a flag by opening the item and opening the Flag menu from the toolbar.

Use the Clear Flag command when you want to remove a flag from an item, and use the Mark Complete command when you want to indicate that you've completed the work flagged for follow-up.

Using Reminders

For new appointments and meeting requests, a reminder is set by default for 15 minutes. With this setting in place, Outlook notifies you at the appropriate time that the event is about to start.

Reset a reminder if you want a second notification, open the item for more information, or click Dismiss to close this window.

When you set up an appointment or a meeting, you can clear the Reminder check box to turn off a reminder. You can also turn off a reminder for an item already on your calendar, and you can adjust the timing of reminders, selecting from a group of preset values between 0 minutes and 2 weeks.

In response to a reminder that Outlook displays, take one of the following steps:

- Click Dismiss to close the reminder.

- Click Open Item to display the item you're being reminded about. (For example, you could open a meeting request and send a message to the organizer if you're running late.)

- Click Dismiss All if more than one item is listed.

- Reset the timing of the reminder, and click Snooze.

You can also set up reminders for task items. (Reminders are not set by default for tasks.) In the task item, select the Reminder check box and then specify the date and time when you want Outlook to display a reminder.

➤ To create a category

1. Switch to Task view (or open a contact item, e-mail message, or appointment item).
2. Click the **Apply Categories** button, and then click **Manage Categories**.
3. In the **Manage Categories** dialog box, click **Create New Category**.
4. Type a name for the category, and select the color you want to associate it with (or use no color).
5. Click **OK**.

➤ To assign an item to a category

1. Open the item, and click the **Apply Categories** button on the toolbar.
2. Select the check box for the category or categories you want to apply to this item.
3. Click away from the menu to close it.

➤ To flag an item

1. In the item list, double-click the item to open it. (For e-mail messages and tasks, you can work with an item in the item list itself.)
2. On the toolbar, click the **Flag** button, and then select the follow-up period you want to apply.
3. Select **Set Date and Reminder** to set up a reminder for the flagged item.

➤ To set up a reminder

1. For an appointment, meeting request, or task item, specify the date and time for a reminder. (For a task item, be sure you select the **Reminder** check box.)
2. When Outlook displays a reminder, do one of the following:
   - Reset the reminder time, and click **Snooze**.
   - Click **Dismiss** to close the reminder.

○   Click **Dismiss All** to close a reminder related to more than one item.

○   Click **Open Item** to view the item associated with the reminder. (If more than one item is listed, select that item and then click **Open Item**.)

Switching Calendar Views

You can display your calendar in the Daily, Weekly, Work Week, or Monthly view. The Daily view is the default view. To switch to a different view, click the button on the menu bar for the view you want.

> **See Also** In the Options dialog box, you can specify different working days and working hours and make other changes to the appearance of your calendar. For details, see "Calendar Settings" later in this chapter.

➤ **To change the calendar view**

→   On the toolbar, click the button for the view you want to see: **Day view**, **Work Week view**, **Week view**, or **Month view**.

Practice Tasks

Practice the skills you learned in this section by performing the following tasks in Outlook Web App:

- Switch to the different calendar views to see the information Outlook displays in each.

- Create a new calendar, and then add several appointments to it. Share this calendar with a colleague or coworker.

- Publish the calendar you created to the Internet, and then send the link to a coworker, friend, or colleague.

- Use the Scheduling Assistant to set up a meeting with other people in your organization.

- Create a category for one or more of your work projects, and then assign items to that category.

- Apply a follow-up flag to a task that is due in two weeks, and set a reminder for one week from today.

2.3 Manage Contacts

To send an e-mail message or a meeting request to someone in your organization, you can use the global address book (also called the *shared address book*). But you will also want to be in touch with people outside your organization. You use Contacts view to create an address book for contacts of your own or to add a contact to an existing address book.

You can store a wide range of information about contacts—from only a name and e-mail address to phone numbers, a street address, and details such as birthdate and the name of an assistant. You can build a contact list by importing information from another e-mail program and create contact groups to facilitate communication with the members of the group. The following sections cover these and other details about working with contacts.

Adding Contacts

The form you use to set up a new contact is organized into four sections: Profile, Contact, Addresses, and Details. You can enter some or all the information you want to store about the contact and then add the contact to your list.

Build a personal address book by adding contact items.

Click New, Contact in the toolbar to open the contact form. (As with other types of items, you can press Ctrl+N to open a blank contact form.) The Profile section includes fields for the contact's name, company, and department; how you want to file the contact (some of the options are LastFirst, First Last, and Company); and other details related to the contact's work environment. Use the Contact section for phone numbers, e-mail addresses, and the contact's website. The Addresses section provides fields for storing three addresses—business, home, and other. Use the list at the top of this section if you want to designate which of these to use as the contact's mailing address. In the Details section, you can add notes about the contact or include a file attachment—anything from a resume to a sales proposal.

> **Tip** You can send an e-mail message to a contact by clicking New Message To Contact on the contact item toolbar. This command is also available when you right-click a contact in the contact list. On this menu, use the Chat command to communicate with the contact in real time.

Use the links at the top of the contact form to jump to the section you want to view. To add this contact to a category, select the category by using the Category button on the toolbar.

> **See Also** For more information about categories, see "Using Categories, Flags, and Reminders" earlier in this chapter.

Adding External Contacts

Office 365 administrators can add external contacts (people who don't use your e-mail domain) to your organization's shared address book. Setting up external contacts is helpful if more than one person in your organization regularly communicates with these contacts.

> ➤ **To add a contact**

1. Click **Contacts** in the navigation pane to display Contacts view.
2. On the toolbar, click **New**, **Contact**.
3. Enter details about the contact, including name, e-mail address, street address, and so on.
4. Click **Save and Close**.

Editing Contact Information

When you need to edit contact information, double-click the contact entry in the list or right-click the contact entry and choose Open. Outlook Web App displays the contact form, and you can add and update the information you need to.

➤ To edit contact information

1. In the contacts list, double-click the contact.

2. Update and add information to the fields in the contact form.

3. Click **Save and Close**.

Deleting a Contact

When you want to remove a contact from Outlook Web App, highlight the contact in the list and then click the Delete button on the toolbar. You can also right-click the contact entry and choose Delete or select the contact and press the Delete key.

> **Important** You cannot undo the action of deleting a contact.

➤ To delete a contact

→ In the contacts list, select the contact and then click the **Delete** button on the toolbar.

Forwarding Contact Information

You can attach a contact item to an e-mail message as a way to distribute the contact's information to others. To begin this operation, either right-click the entry for the contact and choose Forward As Attachment or select the contact entry and then click the Forward link in the reading pane.

As a result of either action, you'll see a message item with the contact information contained in an attachment. Address the message, add any explanation that should accompany the message, and then send it.

➤ To forward contact information

1. Right-click the contact entry, and then choose **Forward As Attachment**.

2. In the e-mail message item, add addresses for recipients, type a subject and message body, and then click **Send**.

Creating Groups and Distribution Lists

By creating a contact group or distribution list, you can send messages or arrange meetings by addressing an item to the group or list rather than to individuals. Contact groups are available only to the person who sets them up. Distribution groups, also called *public groups*, are added to the shared address book and can be used by people within your organization.

Create a Group

A contact group can contain as members people listed in the shared (global) address book, people from your personal contact list, and others. To create a group, click New, Group on the toolbar in Contact view. In the dialog box that Outlook displays, type a name for the group and then click Members to open the address book. In the address book, select the entries for people you want to include in the group and click Members at the bottom of the address book. Use the Show Other Address List link to display additional names, or use the entries under Contacts in the dialog box's navigation pane to display your own contacts lists. When you have added each person you want to include in the group, click OK. When you see the new group window again, click Add To Group.

> **Tip** You can also type the names of contacts in the Members box and then click Add To Group. Separate contacts names with semicolons.

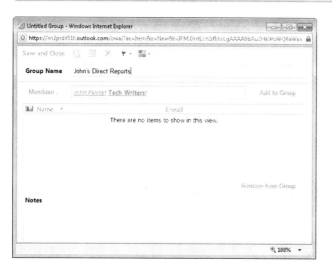

Use this window to name a contact group and define its members. Contact groups are included only in your contacts list.

Before you save and close the new group window, add a note that describes the group and its membership. You can also use the toolbar at the top of this window to send an e-mail message or a meeting request to the group, but you need to save the group before you perform these operations. If you are using categories to classify contacts, assign this group to a category as well.

Setting Up a Distribution List

You can set up a distribution list (also called a *public group*) that becomes an entry in the shared address book. Start by clicking Options, See All Options at the top-right corner of the Outlook Web App window. On the Options page, click Groups. In the window Outlook displays, you can see any public groups you already belong to and any public groups you own (which means you created the public group or have been designated an owner).

> **Important** This section is based on a standard user setting up a public group in the enterprise version of Office 365. Administrators can set up distribution lists from the administration page and have other options for managing memberships.

Under Public Groups I Own, click New. In the New Group window, fields are organized in four sections—General, Ownership, Membership, and Membership Approval. An asterisk marks the required fields. For example, you must enter a display name for the list and an alias, which is combined with your domain name to create an e-mail address for the list. (You can change how the alias appears in the e-mail address if you want to.) Also, add a description for this list so that other users know its purpose.

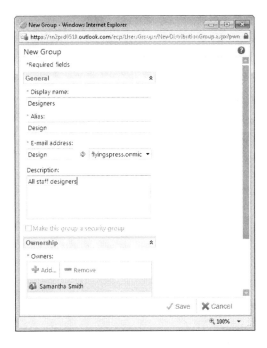

Public groups are included in your organization's address book. Group owners can manage requests to join or leave the group.

In the Ownership area, you'll see your name listed as the distribution list's default owner. To designate other owners, click Add to open the Select Owner dialog box. Select the person or persons you want to add as owners, click Add at the bottom of the dialog box, and then click OK.

In the Membership area, use the Add button to open the Select Members dialog box. Owners of the distribution list are included as members by default, but owners aren't required to be members. Clear the check box for Add Group Owners As Members to remove owners from the group.

In the Membership Approval area, you specify an option for how you want to manage requests to join the group. The default choice is Open, which allows anyone to join— approval of a group owner is not required. If you choose Closed, requests to join are rejected automatically; only group owners can add new members. The third option is Owner Approval. If you select this option, the group owner or owners receive an e-mail requesting approval to join the group, which the owner can approve or reject.

> **See Also** You'll learn more about joining or leaving public groups later in this chapter.

➤ **To create a contact group**

1. On the toolbar, click **New**, **Group**.
2. In the new group window, type a name for the group.
3. In the **Members** box, type the e-mail address or names of contacts you want to add to this group. Separate the entries with a semicolon. (Click **Members** to open the address book to select the contacts and coworkers you want to include in the group.)
4. Click **Add to Group**.
5. Optionally, add a note describing the group, assign the group to a category, or apply a follow-up flag to the group.
6. Click **Save and Close**.

➤ **To create a public group**

1. At the top-right corner of the Outlook Web App window, click **Options**, **See All Options**.
2. On the **Options** page, click **Groups**.
3. Under **Public Groups I Own**, click **New**.
4. In the **New Group** dialog box, type a name, alias, and description for the group.

5. In the **Ownership** area, click **Add** to designate other owners for the group.

6. In the **Membership** area, click **Add** to select the members of the group.

7. In the **Membership Approval** area, select the option you want to use to manage how people can join the group.

Importing Contacts

If you maintain an active contacts list in Microsoft Outlook or another e-mail program, you can import those contacts into Outlook Web App. You should first export the contact list you want to use in Outlook Web App and save the exported file as a .csv file. (CSV is an abbreviation for comma-separated values. Spreadsheet programs such as Microsoft Excel support this format.)

> **Tip** You can also create a contacts list yourself in Excel, for example, and list contact details under column headings such as First Name, Last Name, E-Mail Address, and so on. Save this file as a .csv file and then import the list into Outlook Web App.

You can find plenty of help and information about this task in Office 365 and Outlook Web App. Under Resources on the home page, click How To Import Your Contacts in the Resources list. On the Outlook Web App Options page, click Import Your Contacts From An Existing E-Mail Account in the list of shortcuts.

To import the list, switch to Contacts view and then click Import on the toolbar. In the Import Contacts dialog box, browse to the .csv file with your contacts list, click Open, and then click Next. If Outlook Web App does not encounter any problems, it notifies you that the list was imported successfully and shows how many contacts were imported.

> **Tip** If the same contact is in your Contacts folder and in the .csv file, a duplicate contact will be created.

➤ **To import your contacts**

1. In **Contacts** view, click **Import** on the toolbar.

2. In the **Import Contacts** dialog box, click **Browse**, locate the .csv file containing the contacts you want to import, and then click **Next**.

3. Click **Finish** if the import is successful.

Searching Contacts

To locate a group or individual in your contact list, you can type that contact's name, a portion of the name, or some or all of the text in another contact field. For example, if you type **Jo**, the search results include, for example, contacts named Joe, John, and Josh as well as group names that contain these characters. If you wanted to find all your contacts who work for Adventure Works, you can type **Adventure**.

For contacts, the search scopes you can set are shown in the menu that appears when you click the down arrow at the right end of the search box. Choose from This Folder, This Folder And Subfolders, and Search All Contact Items. By default, contact searches occur within the current folder. Choose Set Default Location on this menu, and select a different setting if you want to.

You can also search for a contact by category. Click the double down arrow at the right side of the search box, select the check box for Category, and then choose the category you want to search in.

➤ **To search for a contact**

1. In the search box at the top of the contact list, type the text you want to search for.
2. Click the search button, or press Enter.

Practice Tasks

Practice the skills you learned in this section by performing the following tasks in Outlook Web App:

- If you have not yet done so, import a contacts list you work with into Outlook Web App.
- Add two contacts to your list.
- Create a public group, and set the membership permission so that requests to join the group are sent to you (as the group owner).
- Search for contacts using last names and company names.

2.4 Manage Tasks

Setting up tasks to keep track of what you need to do can be as simple as recording the name of a task. Using this approach, you can use Tasks view to manage your to-do list. By adding details to a task—a due date, task status, and priority, for example—you develop a tool that can help you manage workflow, track hours you need to bill, and document issues that are affecting your progress in completing a task.

Creating Tasks

The steps you take to create a task depend on the level of detail you want to enter at the start. To enter just a task name and (optionally) a due date, use the task list. To add more details when you create a task, open a new task item.

Adding a Task from the Task List

For tasks that require only a name and possibly a due date, switch to Tasks view and use the text box at the top of the task list to enter the task name and specify a due date. (You can add a task without specifying a due date). Click the Add New Task button at the right of this text box (or press Enter), and the task is added to the list.

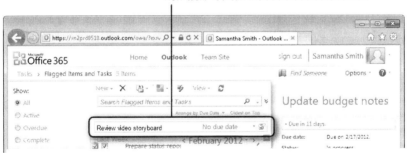

Use the text box above the task list to enter a new task. You can include a due date as well.

Using the New Task Item Window

To set up a new task with additional details, click New in the menu bar. (You can also press Ctrl+N when in Task view.) You generally won't enter all the information for a task when you create it this way, but in most cases you will at least specify the subject of the task; enter information such as the start and due dates, its priority, and an initial status; and set up a reminder for when the task next needs your attention.

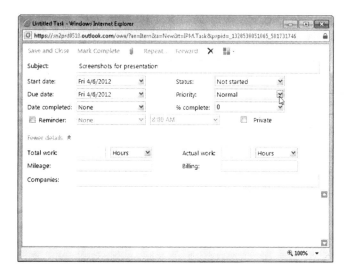

Creating a task by using a task item lets you specify initial details such as status and priority.

By default, the status of new tasks is set to Not Started. If your work on this task won't begin immediately, keep this setting. You can change the task's status to In Progress if work has commenced, or you can choose Waiting On Others if your work on this task is dependent on other tasks assigned to you or tasks your colleagues or coworkers need to complete.

> **Tip** The Deferred status mostly applies in situations in which work on a project is suspended or delayed because other tasks have higher priority or resources aren't available.

For priority, you can keep the default Normal setting or select Low or High when you want to rank this task within the set of tasks you're tracking.

> **See Also** You can associate a task with a category by choosing the category from the toolbar. For more details, see "Using Categories, Flags, and Reminders" earlier in this chapter.

You can add an attachment to a task item. For example, you might attach the draft of meeting minutes or a status report you need to review and formalize. If you don't want other people to see this task on a calendar you've shared, select Private.

> **See Also** For information about sharing calendars, see "Setting Up Shared Calendars and Managing Permissions" earlier in this chapter.

Setting Up Repeating Tasks

For some tasks—such as the submission of weekly status reports or other recurring work—you want to set up the task so that your task list includes an entry for each time the task is due. First, click Repeat in the toolbar to open the Repetition dialog box, and then select how often this task recurs (daily, weekly, and so on). The fields on the right side of the Repeat Pattern section change to correspond with your selection. The following screen shots show the details for tasks that repeat weekly and monthly.

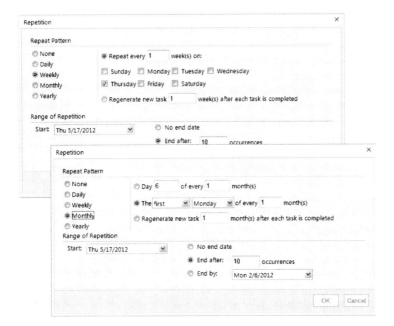

Set up recurring tasks, appointments, and meetings using settings in this dialog box.

Complete the Repeat Pattern portion of the dialog box by specifying whether the task repeats every week or every two weeks, for example. Choose the day or days of the week the task is due on, and enter a value for how often Outlook should generate a new task item.

The Range Of Repetition section provides controls you use to specify start and end dates. You can choose no end date, specify the number of occurrences (for example, six regularly scheduled planning meetings), or indicate the date on which the recurring task ends, which might correspond with a project's completion date.

➤ **To create a task from the task list**

1. At the top of the task list, type a new task, and specify a due date if needed.

2. Click **Add New Task**.

➤ **To set up a new task item**

1. On the toolbar, click **New**, **Task**.

2. In the task window, type a subject for the task and enter information such as the start date, due date, status, and priority.

3. Specify the date and time when you want to be reminded of this task.

4. Click **Save and Close**.

➤ **To define a repeating task**

1. On the task window's toolbar, click **Repeat**.

2. In the **Repetition** dialog box, choose the option for how often the task recurs (**Daily**, **Weekly**, **Monthly**, **Yearly**).

3. Fill in the corresponding details in the **Repeat Pattern** fields. For example, select the day or days of the week that a weekly task is due.

4. In the **Range of Repetition** area, specify a start date and choose an option for when the repeating task is scheduled to end.

Updating Task Information

For some tasks you track, you need only to create the task item, specify a due date, and then mark the task complete when it's done. (See the next section for details on how to mark a task complete.) For other tasks, especially those with a long duration, you need to keep the information in the task item current so that you can monitor how much work is complete and maintain a clear view of which tasks have high priority. You can also use a task item to record information about billable hours, for example, and record notes about your progress or any issues that need resolution.

> **Tip** You can use the Show options on the navigation pane to filter the task list when you need to update a series of tasks. For more details, see Chapter 1, "Navigating Office 365."

To update task information, double-click the task item in the task list (or right-click the task item and choose Open). You can then update the Status field, for example, from Not Started to Waiting For Others, Deferred, or In Progress. If necessary, reset the task's priority, changing it from Normal to High if this task now needs more or all of your time. Update the Due Date field if this task's schedule has changed.

Use the % Complete field to indicate how much of the work is behind you. (If you specify a value for % Complete for a task whose status is set to Not Started, the status is reset to In Progress automatically.) You can choose one of the preset values in this list or type a different percentage.

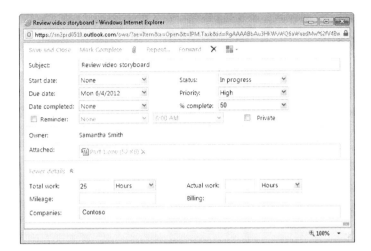

As you work on a task, you can update the status, priority, and percent complete and enter details such as hours worked.

At this point, you might also enter or update details about the total work and actual hours you've spent on the task, specify mileage or billing details, or add notes or attachments related to the task.

> **Tip** You cannot edit task details in the reading pane, but you can set a reminder for the task or mark the task as a private task.

➤ To update task information

1. In the task list, right-click a task and choose **Open**.

2. Specify current values for fields such as **Due Date**, **Status**, **Priority**, and **% Complete**.

3. Add notes or other details about work on the task.

4. Click **Save and Close**.

Marking Tasks Complete

When you finish your work on a task, you have several ways in which you can mark the task complete.

> **Tip** Marking the current instance of a repeating task complete is the trigger for Outlook Web App to generate a new instance of the task.

- Select the check box to the left of the task's entry in the task list.
- Select the task in the task list, and click Mark Complete on the toolbar.
- Open the task item, and click Mark Complete on the toolbar.

- Open the task item, and specify a value for Date Completed.
- Open the task item, and choose Completed from the Status field.
- Open the task item, and specify 100 in the % Complete field.

Following any of these steps updates other relevant fields. For example, clicking Mark Complete changes Date Completed to the current date, Status to Completed, and % Complete to 100.

➤ To mark a task complete

1. Select the task in the task list.
2. On the toolbar, click **Mark Complete**.

Practice Tasks

Practice the skills you learned in this section by performing the following tasks in Outlook Web App:

- Set up three tasks from the task list.
- Open a new task item, enter task details, and then define this task as a monthly repeating task that ends after eight occurrences.
- For two of the tasks you defined, mark the tasks complete by using either the task list, the % Complete field, or the Date Completed field.

2.5 Configure Outlook Web App Options

The following sections describe the options you can set to manage your work in Outlook Web App and customize how Outlook behaves. These options are included in a series of pages and categories you can display by clicking Options under Outlook on the Office 365 portal's home page or by clicking Options in the Outlook window.

Viewing Account Options

On the Account page, you work with settings for your Office 365 account and can also connect other e-mail accounts you have to Office 365.

My Account

Under My Account on the Account page, Outlook displays information such as your display name and user ID, how much space you've used in your mailbox, and contact information. To enter or change account information, click Edit.

If you want to access your Office 365 e-mail account from an e-mail client that supports the POP, IMAP, or SMTP protocol, click the link below the list of contact phone numbers to display the settings to use.

You can also find here a list of shortcuts to common tasks, including changing your password and forwarding e-mail.

Connected Accounts

Click Connected Accounts on the Account page to tie your Office 365 account to another e-mail account and view the messages sent to that account in Outlook. You can also specify an account to which to forward e-mail sent to your Office 365 account.

To set up a connected account, enter the e-mail address and the password associated with that account. Outlook Web App searches for the account and connects the accounts if the account and password match. When you click Finish in the New Account Creation Wizard, messages from the connected account start downloading to Outlook Web App. After messages (and the folder structure) of the connected account are downloaded, the status for the account should indicate OK.

In the list of connected accounts, select an account and click the Delete button to remove the connection. Deleting a connection does not remove messages already downloaded, but new messages sent to that account won't show up in Outlook Web App. Click Details to view the current status, display name (which you can modify), and other account information.

Use the Default Reply Address list to specify whether you want to use a specific address for all replies. Keep the default setting (Automatic) if you want to reply using the address of the account a message was sent to.

Under Forwarding, enter the e-mail address to which you want to forward your Office 365 messages. Clear the option to keep a copy of messages in Outlook Web App if that's your preference. Click Start Forwarding to activate this feature. Click Stop Forwarding to deactivate this process.

> ### To set up a connected account

1. On the **Account** page, click **Connected Accounts**.

2. Under **Connected Accounts**, click **New**.

3. Type the e-mail address and password for the account you want to connect to, and then click **Next**.

4. If the connection is made successfully, click **Finish**.

> ### To forward e-mail messages

1. On the **Account** page, click **Connected Accounts**.

2. In the **Forwarding** area at the bottom of the page, type the address for the e-mail account you want to forward messages to.

3. Click **Start Forwarding**.

Organizing E-mail

In addition to creating folders on the navigation pane for sorting and storing messages, you can use the options under Organize E-Mail to create inbox rules and automatic replies, view delivery information about messages you've sent and received, and select retention policies, which are rules set up to delete or archive messages after a specified period of time.

> **See Also** Refer to "Using Inbox Rules" earlier in this chapter for details about how to set up and manage inbox rules.

Sending an Automatic Reply

When you are out of the office and away from e-mail, create an automatic reply that senders receive to notify them of your absence, tell them how they might otherwise reach you, or direct them to your manager or a colleague if they need assistance while you're away.

Display the Automatic Replies page under Organize E-Mail. Enable automatic replies, and then use the text boxes and formatting tools to create the message senders will receive. Use the calendar controls to define a time period for which the automatic reply is active. Otherwise, the reply is active until you return to this page and select Do Not Send Automatic Replies.

You can create one automatic reply for people within your organization and a different message for people on the outside. You can clear the option to send the reply to external senders (people not in your organization) or control the scope of your external reply by switching from the option Send Replies To All External Senders to the option Send Replies Only To Senders In My Contacts List.

> ➤ **To set up an automatic reply**

1. On the **Organize E-Mail** page, click **Automatic Replies**.

2. Select **Send automatic replies**.

3. To define a specific time period for the reply, select **Send replies only during this time period** and then use the calendar controls to specify a date and time.

4. Type and format the message you want to send to people in your organization.

5. If you do not want to send an automatic reply to people outside your organization, clear the check box for this option. If you retain this setting, select the option you want to use for who to send replies to—all external senders or only senders in your contacts list.

6. Type and format the message for external contacts.

7. Click **Save**.

Viewing Delivery Reports

Delivery reports provide delivery details about messages you send or receive. For example, you can see that a message was delivered to a recipient and when.

On the Delivery Reports page, select the option to search for messages you sent or messages you received, and then use the Select Users link to identify the sender or recipient. You can choose more than one name. You can also search by words in the subject line. After you click Search, Outlook displays matching results. Select an item in the list and then click Details to view more information. You can use the column headings (From, To, and so on) to sort the results list.

> ➤ **To view a delivery report**

1. On the **Organize E-Mail** page, click **Delivery Reports**.

2. Enter the criteria for messages you want to search for (sender, recipient, or text in the subject line), and then click **Search**.

3. In the **Search Results** list, select a message and then click **Details** to view the delivery report details.

Specifying Retention Policies

As the volume of e-mail grows and items age, you can turn to retention policies to automatically delete messages after a specified period of time or to add them to an archive.

Click Add on the Retention Policies page to select a policy you want to apply. The following screen shot shows the options available in the Office 365 enterprise plan. Most of these are straightforward. The seventh item—Personal 1 Year Move To Archive—means that items are moved to an archive mailbox after one year.

Specify a retention policy to let Outlook automatically delete or archive messages.

If an Office 365 administrator has defined custom retention policies, those policies are listed in this dialog box as well. Select the policy or policies you want to apply to your mailbox, and then click Add. Click Save to retain the settings.

> ➤ **To specify a retention policy**

1. On the **Organize E-Mail** page, click **Retention Policies**.

2. Click **Add**.

3. In the **Select Retention Policy** dialog box, select a policy (or policies), click **Add**, and then click **Save**.

Using Groups

Earlier in this chapter, in the section "Creating Groups and Distribution Lists," you learned how to set up a public group of your own. You also use the Groups page to join or leave a group that you belong to. Whether you can join or leave a group on your own depends on the settings specified for membership approval. (See the earlier section for more details.)

To add yourself to a group, click Join, select the group in the window Outlook displays, and then click Join. (You can view more information about the group before you join it by clicking Details.) If enrollment is open, you are added to the group. If you need approval to join a group, you'll see a message indicating that a request for you to join was sent to the group owner, and you'll receive a reply telling you whether you've been approved or not after the group owner takes action on your request.

Whether you can leave a group on your own also depends on membership approval settings. If you can't leave a group, you'll receive a message indicating that. You should contact the group owner to request that the owner remove you from the group.

➤ **To join or leave a public group**

1. Click **Groups** on the **Options** page.

2. Under **Public Groups I Belong To**, select a group and click **Leave** to remove yourself from the group.

   You'll receive a confirmation if you can leave the group on your own or an indication that the membership departure is closed if you can't.

3. Click **Join** to see a list of groups in the address book.

4. In the dialog box, select the group and then click **Join**.

   Outlook confirms that you've been added to the group, displays a message indicating a request has been sent to the owner, or displays a message that group membership is closed. If you see this message, contact the group owner directly with your request.

Changing Outlook Settings

Defining an e-mail signature, managing conversations and e-mail notifications, and changing calendar views are some of the tasks you can perform on the Settings page of the Options window. Use the buttons at the top of the Settings page (Mail, Spelling, Calendar, General, and Regional) to display the options you want to work with.

Mail Settings

Under Mail, you can set the following options:

- **E-Mail Signature**   Type your signature in the text box. Use the toolbar to add formatting such as bold and italics, switch to a different font, apply highlighting, and so on. The toolbar includes Undo and Redo buttons. You can also include a variety of hyperlinks in your signature. Open the Hyperlink dialog box by clicking Insert Hyperlink and then choose an entry from the Type list. The default type is HTTP, for a URL on the Internet or your intranet. Choose Mailto if you want to include a link to your e-mail address.

  You can insert your signature when you create a message or select the option to include it automatically.

- **Message Format**   Options in this area control whether the Bcc and From fields are shown on messages. You can also choose the default message format to use, either HTML or plain text, and set up the default message font if you are using the HTML format. Plain text messages are composed in Times New Roman.

- **Message Options**   The first option in this group lets you specify what Outlook should do when you move or delete a message item. The default setting is Open The Next Item, but you can change this to Open The Previous Item or Return To The View.

  The next four options control message notifications. By default, Outlook plays a sound when you receive a message (including a meeting request) and notifies you when you receive new e-mail, voice mail, or a fax. The last option in this group, which is not selected by default, controls whether Outlook empties the Deleted Items folder when you sign out.

- **Read Receipts**   By default, if you receive a message for which the sender requested a read receipt, Outlook prompts you to send a response. You can change the read-receipt setting so that Outlook sends a response automatically or never sends a response.

- **Reading Pane**   Unread messages are indicated in bold type in the message list, which lets you identify these messages at a glance. When you review messages with the reading pane open, Outlook by default marks a message as read when you select it in the message list. You can turn off this feature by selecting Don't Automatically Mark Items As Read. You can also control the period of time Outlook waits before marking the message that's displayed in the reading pane as read. This setting is helpful if you want to use the reading pane to scan messages (selecting them one by one in the message list) but don't want Outlook to mark the messages as read when you select them. The default interval is 5 seconds.

- **Conversations** The options in this area control how messages in a conversation are sorted. In the reading pane, messages in a conversation are usually sorted with the newest message on top. You can switch this order by selecting Newest Message On Bottom. In the message list, messages in an expanded conversation are, by default, sorted to match the order set for the reading pane. You can change this setting to Show The Conversation Tree if you want to display the messages in that order. The last option in this area lets you hide deleted items from the list of items shown in a conversation.

Spelling Settings

Outlook Web App includes a few selected spelling options. You can select options so that the spelling checker ignores words in uppercase and words with numbers. You can also specify that spelling is checked automatically before you send a message. If you want to use a different dictionary to check spelling, select the dictionary from the list provided.

Calendar Settings

Settings for your calendar include those that control which hours are shown as your working hours, how Outlook processes meeting requests, how and when reminders are displayed, and text message notifications sent to your phone.

- **Appearance** Use the first set of options in this area to specify which days of the week are shown as your work week (the default configuration is Monday through Friday) and your working hours (8 a.m. to 5 p.m. is the default selection). You can also specify a different day as the first day of the week, show time in 15-minute increments instead of the default 30-minute setting, and also select an option to show week numbers when you display your calendar in Month view.

- **Text Messaging Notifications** If you want to receive text messages on your mobile phone to remind you of meetings and other updates to your calendar, click Set Up Notifications and step through the wizard to secure the passcode you need. After notifications are set up, select the options for receiving notifications. Options are available for calendar updates and meeting requests. Both of these options let you restrict the time when you receive notifications to your working hours. You can also choose to receive a daily calendar agenda at the time you specify.

  If you need to make adjustments to the settings for notifications—for example, if you change to a different mobile carrier or number—click the link at the bottom of this section.

- **Reminders**   In this area, clear the option Show Reminder Alerts if you don't want to see reminders, or clear Play A Sound When A Reminder Is Due if you want to receive a reminder, but silently. You can change the default time period for a reminder, which is initially set to 15 minutes before an appointment occurs.

- **Automatic Processing**   The four settings in this area control how Outlook processes meeting requests, responses to meeting requests, and notifications about requests that are forwarded. By default, meeting requests are added to your calendar and marked as Tentative. To have more control over your calendar, clear this option.

General Settings

The first area on this page provides settings for how e-mail names are resolved when you check names. By default, Outlook looks first in the global address list. You can change the setting for this option to your Contacts folder.

Under Accessibility, select the check box for Use The Blind And Low Vision Experience. You need to sign out of Office 365 and then sign in again for this setting to take effect.

Regional Settings

Under Regional Settings, you specify which language, date and time formats, and time zone to use. The language you select determines the options for date and time formats. You can then choose from the available formats.

➤ To specify Outlook settings

1. On the **Options** page, click **Settings**.

2. Use the icons at the top of the page to display the settings you want to work with.

3. Click **Save** to preserve the settings you select and change.

Using Your Mobile Phone with Outlook Web App

If you have a compatible mobile phone, you can configure the phone to work with Office 365. By doing this, you can use your phone to view e-mail and voice messages sent to your inbox, entries on your calendar, your contacts, and task data. To gain access to all this information via your phone, your phone must support Exchange ActiveSync, which most current mobile phones do. If the phone you have doesn't support Exchange ActiveSync, you can still set up the phone so that you can use it to send and receive e-mail using your Office 365 account.

You can use a wizard to help guide you in setting up your phone. Switch to the Phone page in the Outlook Web App Options dialog box. Under Mobile Phones, click the link provided to display a Help topic that summarizes the requirements for synchronizing a phone with Outlook. On that page, click the link for the Mobile Phone Setup Wizard to begin.

The wizard asks for two items of input: your mobile phone operating system (iOS for an iPhone and Windows Phone are examples) and the type of configuration you want. If you select Android as your operating system, for example, the choices in the What Would You Like To Do list let you set up Microsoft Exchange e-mail on your phone or set up your phone using the POP or IMAP e-mail protocol. The wizard uses the selections you make in these lists to display a set of steps for how you set up your phone and find the appropriate server. For example, to set up a Windows Phone, you might only need to add an account for Outlook and enter your e-mail address and password. With this information, your phone can be configured automatically. If automatic configuration does not work, you'll find the detailed steps to follow.

Several of the options include videos that show you the configuration steps. You can also consult the Mobile Phone Setup Reference (a link is provided on the page where you start the wizard) for more details about the phone you have and its capabilities for interacting with your Office 365 e-mail account.

You also use the Mobile Phones page to manage the phone or phones you've connected to Office 365. You can view the details for the device, block your phone if you happen to lose it, see the sync status, and access other information.

The Phones page also includes settings for setting up text-messaging notifications for your phone (similar to the options available under Calendar on the Settings page). Use the Turn On Notifications link to set up notifications. You need to specify your locale, which mobile carrier you use, and your mobile phone number. Office 365 generates a passcode and sends this information to you in a text message. When you receive it, enter it in the text box provided to complete the setup process.

After text message notifications are active, use the Calendar Notifications link to specify the types of notifications you want to receive and when you want to receive them. Use the e-mail notifications link to set up an inbox rule for managing the text messages you receive.

> **See Also** For more information about inbox rules, see "Using Inbox Rules" earlier in this chapter.

➤ **To set up your mobile phone to work with Office 365**

1. Under **Mobile Phones** on the **Phone** page, click the link **Configure the phone to synchronize with Microsoft Exchange**.

2. Review the general information about phone compatibility, and then click **Mobile Phone Setup Wizard**.

3. On the **Mobile Phone Setup Wizard** page, select your phone's operating system and the type of configuration you want to use.

4. Follow the procedures provided for your device.

➤ **To set up text-messaging notifications**

1. Under **Text Messaging** on the **Phone** page, click **Turn On Notifications**.

2. Specify your locale, mobile provider, and mobile number to receive the required passcode.

3. Enter the passcode when you receive it, and then click **Finish**.

4. Use the links provided to specify how you want to manage notifications for calendar entries and to set up an inbox rule.

Blocking or Allowing Messages

The options under Block And Allow control how Outlook Web App handles junk e-mail. They allow you to build a list of senders and recipients you consider safe and also designate blocked senders. E-mail from blocked senders is always moved directly to the Junk E-Mail folder.

Reduce spam while letting legitimate messages through by
specifying safe senders and those you want to block.

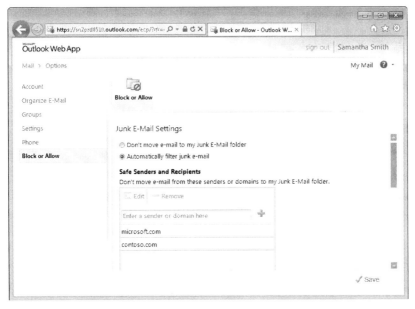

The option Automatically Filter Junk E-Mail is selected by default. This means that
Outlook routes messages that fit certain criteria to your Junk E-Mail folder instead of to
your inbox. If you prefer to manage all messages yourself, select Don't Move E-Mail To
My Junk E-Mail Folder.

By selecting Trust E-Mail From My Contacts, you specify that Outlook should treat any
message from someone listed in your contacts list as safe. You can also add individual
e-mail addresses, as well as domain names (such as contoso.com), to the Safe Senders
And Recipients list. Click the plus sign to add a name you entered to the list. Select a
name in the list and click Edit to change the address, or click Remove to take the name
off the list.

Follow the same general steps to manage the Blocked Senders list. Any message you
receive from an address or domain that's included in this list is moved to the Junk E-Mail
folder.

You can increase the range of messages Outlook doesn't trust by selecting the option at
the bottom of this page—Don't Trust E-Mail Unless It Comes From Someone In My Safe
Senders And Recipients List Or Local Senders. *Local senders* refers to colleagues within
your domain.

> **Tip** In the message list, right-click a message, point to Junk E-Mail, and then choose an option to add the sender to the blocked senders or safe senders list or to add the sender's domain to the safe senders list.

> ### To block and allow messages

1. On the **Options** page, click **Block or Allow**.
2. Enter a sender or domain in the **Safe Senders and Recipients** list, and then click the plus sign.
3. Enter a sender or domain in the **Block Senders** list, and then click the plus sign.
4. Click **Save**.

Practice Tasks

Practice the skills you learned in this section by performing the following tasks in Outlook Web App:

- If you have an additional e-mail account, connect it to Outlook Web App.
- Create an automatic reply for external contacts.
- Use the Calendar settings page to send text message notifications to your mobile phone (if you have one).
- Change the sort order for conversations.
- Add three of your contacts to the Safe Senders And Recipients list.

Objective Review

Before finishing this chapter, be sure you have mastered the following skills:

2.1   Manage e-mail

2.2   Organize calendars

2.3   Manage contacts

2.4   Manage tasks

2.5   Configure Outlook Web App options

3 Collaborating by Using Lync Online

The skills tested in this section of the Microsoft Office exam for Office 365 relate to how you collaborate using Microsoft Lync Online. Specifically, the following objectives are associated with this set of skills:

3.1 Configure Lync options

3.2 Employ collaboration tools and techniques

3.3 Manage Lync contacts

3.4 Use Lync tools

Ease of communication, knowing whether someone is available or in a meeting, and collaborating on content in real time are essential capabilities that Lync provides to users of Office 365. In Lync, you can place calls, send e-mail or instant messages, hold meetings and group conversations, annotate a presentation, and sketch on a whiteboard. In the sections that follow, you'll learn about the skills needed to make use of each of these features and more, how to manage the contacts you communicate with, and about other tools that Lync provides.

3.1 Configure Lync Options

As an introduction to Lync, the first section of this chapter describes the options you can specify for how to work with Lync. To open the Lync Options dialog box, click the Options button to the right of your name. You can also open the dialog box from the Tools menu.

> **Tip** To view the Tools menu, click the arrow next to the Options button. To show the menu bar in the Lync window, click the arrow and then choose Show Menu bar.

General Page

At the top of the General page are options that control the formatting of instant messages. These options control the display of emoticons, the background color in the instant message window, and the font properties of the text you type. Keep the option Show Emoticons In Instant Messages selected if you want to replace specific keyboard combinations—for example, **:)**—with a graphic. In this case, you would see a small smiling face.

In instant message conversations, Lync by default alternates the background color so that you can distinguish elements of the conversation more easily. Clear the check box that controls this option if you want to keep the background a consistent color.

Click Change Font to open a dialog box in which you can select a different font and specify properties such as color, size, and formatting (italics, semibold, bold, and others). The settings you select in the Change Font dialog box affect the text you type but not the text in messages you receive from contacts.

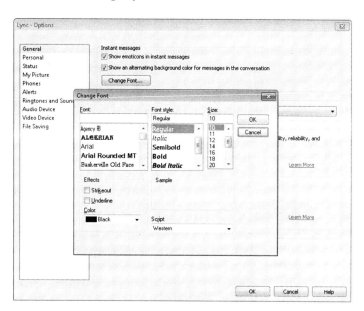

Use the Change Font button to set options for the font you use in instant messages.

Use the other options on the General page to control the following settings:

- If you installed versions of Lync in more than one language, select the language you want to use in this area.

- Microsoft uses its Customer Experience Improvement Program to collect information from users, which Microsoft then analyzes to see how its customers use the features in its software. You can opt in to this program by selecting the option

Allow Microsoft To Collect Information About How I Use Lync. The Learn More link for this option takes you to a page that provides answers to frequently asked questions and tells you more about what Microsoft does with the information it collects and how it protects your privacy.

- Logs are used by system administrators to collect, analyze, and save data. A system administrator might ask you to turn on either of the two logging options to do troubleshooting. Standard users who are not asked to activate these options don't need to be concerned with them.

- When you minimize the Lync application window, the minimized window appears as an item on the Windows task bar by default. You can select the Minimize To The Notification Area Instead Of The Task Bar option in the Application Window area if you prefer that the minimized window appear in the notification area.

Personal Page

Use the Personal page to configure the following options:

- **My Account**   Update the e-mail address you use to sign in to Lync. By default, connection settings for the Lync server that your account is associated with are detected automatically. Click the Advanced button to open a dialog box in which you can choose an option to manually configure connection settings. You need to know the name or IP address for the internal server and external server and whether your connection uses the TCP or TLS connection protocol. These are advanced settings.

  In the My Account area, you can also select or clear options to start Lync when you log on to Windows and to display Lync in the foreground when it starts.

- **Personal Information Manager**   In this area, you can specify how Lync works together with Microsoft Exchange Server or Microsoft Outlook. By default, all the options in this area are selected. With these options set, Lync uses information from your Outlook calendar to display presence and status information, which alerts your Lync contacts whether you are available, in a meeting, or on a call. For example, during the time in which your calendar in Outlook shows that you are busy, your presence in Lync is shown the same way.

  As you'll learn more about later in this chapter, you can set privacy relationships in Lync to specify which of your contacts can view details about meetings and your other activities. You should consider privacy relationships in choosing whether to maintain or clear the option that shows an active out-of-office message to contacts who you've defined with the privacy relationship Family And Friends, Workgroup, or Colleagues.

A record of your instant message conversations and call logs is stored in an Outlook folder named Conversation History. Clear either or both of these options to do without this record.

The final option in this area specifies whether Lync contacts are stored as personal contacts in Exchange.

- **Location**   Depending on how your organization has configured Lync, you can use the option in the Location area to share information about your location with other programs.

- **Display Photo**   If you don't want to see pictures of your contacts, clear this option. If you maintain this option, you'll see thumbnail photographs of the contacts who have posted them.

> **See Also** You'll learn more about posting your own photograph in the section "My Picture Page."

- **Activity Feed**   Activities such as changes in your status, notes you add to Lync, and changes to personal information are displayed in the Activities Feed list for your contacts to see. Clear this option if you want only personal notes and out-of-office messages to be displayed.

Status Page

As mentioned earlier, Lync shows your status on the basis of your activities. Lync also uses a colored presence indicator to let contacts know when you are busy or available. You can change your status to Busy, Away, or Do Not Disturb by choosing an option from the menu that appears under your name in the Lync window.

The settings on the Status page control when Lync changes your status automatically. By default, if your computer remains idle for five minutes, Lync switches your status to Inactive. If your status is Inactive for five minutes, Lync switches your status to Away. Use the options on this page to change the timing of these changes.

You can also select an option through which system settings are overridden and everyone can see your presence. If you don't want to exercise this option, keep the default setting, which leaves this decision to the system administrator.

My Picture Page

You can include a picture that others see as part of your contact information. If your organization has set up a picture directory, you can use an image of yourself stored there. If you don't want to use your standard organizational picture, you can select the option Do Not Show My Picture or point to a picture of yourself that you've stored on a website.

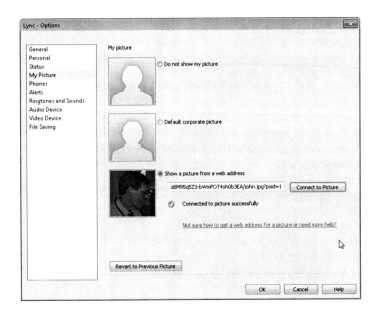

Select the top option if you don't want to display a picture or post a picture of your own. You must post the picture to a web location that doesn't have restricted access.

A picture that you store on a website must be no more than 30 kilobytes (KB). You can right-click the image file and choose Properties to see the image's file size. If you need to resize the picture to make it smaller, open the picture in Windows Photo Editor (or a comparable program) and then use the Snipping Tool (under Accessories on the Start menu) to capture a smaller portion of the image. You can also edit the picture in Paint.

The picture must be stored in a publicly available location on a site such as Windows Live SkyDrive, Facebook, Flickr, or LinkedIn. Once you have the picture uploaded to the site, navigate to the image so that you can copy the image's URL. To find the URL, right-click the image and choose Properties or use a command such as Get Link. Copy the URL, return to the Lync Options dialog box, and then paste the URL into the text box below the option Show A Picture From A Web Address. Click Connect To Picture to check that the URL is correct.

Phones Page

Use the buttons at the top of the Phones page to enter your work, home, mobile, or other phone number. The numbers you provide here are visible on your contact card in Lync, depending on the privacy relationship you've designated for a contact. These numbers are visible to contacts with the Colleagues, Workgroup, or Friends And Family privacy relationships, but they are not visible to contacts you've designated as blocked contacts or external contacts.

Depending on your organization's configuration of Lync, the Phone Integration option might not be enabled.

If you or a contact use Teletype (TTY) because of a hearing impairment, connect a TTY device to your computer and then select this option.

In the Joining Conference Calls area on the Phones page, you can specify how you want to participate in conference calls. By default, the conference call number is set to use Lync (via the Voice over Internet Protocol, or VoIP). You can list a work number as a phone number on this page and then choose which method you want to use during conference calls or online meetings. If you want to be prompted before joining a call, select that option as well.

Alerts Page

The four options on the Alerts page manage when you receive notifications. By default, Lync alerts you when another user adds you to that user's contact list and allows you to add that person to your list. Clear the check box for this option if you don't want to receive this alert.

You can choose one of three options for receiving alerts when your status is set to Do Not Disturb. You can choose not to see any alerts, to see only conversation alerts from people specified as members of your workgroup, or to see all alerts but only conversation alerts from people in your workgroup.

Ringtones And Sounds Page

You can assign one of the built-in ringtones for calls that occur in Lync. Select an entry in the Calls To list and then select the ringtone you want to associate with that item. You'll hear a preview of the ringtone when you select an item in the Ringtone list. Choose None to turn off ringtones.

By default, Lync plays sounds, which include a ringtone for incoming calls and instant messages. Clear the check box for this option if you prefer to hear no sounds from Lync. If you keep this option selected, use the three related options to fine-tune the conditions when Lync plays a sound. For example, Lync mutes sounds for incoming instant messages if you are viewing an instant messaging conversation. Clear this check box if you don't want Lync to mute sounds in this situation.

Also by default, Lync "keeps sounds to a minimum" when your status is set to Do Not Disturb. You can apply this practice to when your status is Busy as well.

If you want to associate specific sounds with events in Lync, click the Sound Settings button to open the Sound dialog box. On the dialog box's Sounds tab, scroll down in the Program Events list until you see Microsoft Lync 2010. Under Lync, you'll see a number of events with which you can associate a sound. The following events are available:

Busy Signal	Incoming Private Line Call
Call Ended	Incoming Response Group Call
Call Error	Income Team Call
Connecting Tone	Muting Tone
Data Sharing Invitation	New Message
Dial Tone	On Hold
Howler	Outgoing Call
Incoming Call	Redirect Call
Incoming Call in Full Screen Mode	Second Incoming Call
Incoming Delegate Call	Status Alert
Incoming Instant Message	Untag

Select an event in the list to see which sound file is currently associated with it. You can switch to a different .wav file or choose None for a particular event.

Audio Device Page

You can control the volume for your speaker, microphone, and ringer on this page. Select the audio device whose settings you want to test or change. Use the buttons in the Speaker and Ringer areas to test the volume, and use the slider to adjust the volume if you need to. For the microphone setting, speak at the volume you would for a meeting or a call. The volume bar moves as you speak more softly or more loudly.

Use the Also Ring check box under Secondary Ringer if you want to activate that feature. If you select a secondary ringer, you can choose the option to have Lync unmute the ringer when your phone rings.

Video Device Page

If you have a webcam connected to your computer, you can provide a video feed during calls and online meetings you hold in Lync. You use the Video Device page to configure the settings for the webcam. Select a webcam and then click Webcam Settings.

The Properties dialog box Lync displays depends on the type of webcam you have. As an example, for a Microsoft LifeCam, you see a dialog box with the tabs Camera Control and Video Settings. Options on the Camera Control tab affect focus, zoom, pan, and tilt. You need to clear the Auto check box to make changes to the setting for focus. Click Default to return the settings on this tab to their default values.

The Video Settings tab's options affect brightness, white balance, and saturation. These options will depend on the webcam you have.

> **Important** Your webcam must be connected to work with the options on this page. Be sure to view the webcam image as you work with these settings so that you can see how your changes are applied to the resolution and the quality of the video.

File Saving Page

During meetings and calls you hold using Lync, you can exchange files as attachments. Lync also has a built-in feature that lets you record calls and meetings, which you can then play back or publish for others to see.

> **See Also** For more information about recording meetings and managing recordings, see "Holding Web Conferences" and "Using Recording Manager" later in this chapter.

The File Saving page shows the path to where Lync stores files you receive in Lync and the recordings you make of conversations. For file transfers, the default location is C:\Users*username*\Documents\My Received Files. For Lync recordings, the default location is C:\Users*username*\Lync Recordings. Use the Browse buttons to open a dialog box in which you can select a different folder for one or both of these settings.

Before Lync changes the path for recordings, it displays a message prompting you to confirm the action. Lync takes this extra step to alert you that choosing not to store recordings in the default location makes the recordings available to people with access to the folder you choose.

➤ **To open the Options dialog box**

➔ In the Lync window, click the **Options** button to the right of your name.

Or

➔ Click the arrow to the right of the **Options** button, point to **Tools**, and then click **Options**.

➤ **To turn off instant message conversation history**

1. In the **Lync Options** dialog box, click the **Personal** page.

2. Clear the option **Save my instant message conversations in my email Conversation History folder.**

➤ **To add a picture**

1. In the **Lync Options** dialog box, click the **My Picture** page.

2. Choose the option you want to use—to display no picture, the default picture from your organization, or a picture you post on the Web.

3. If you select the third option, post the picture in a publicly available site (such as Windows Live SkyDrive or Facebook).

4. Copy the URL that points to the picture, and then copy that URL into the **Lync Options** dialog box.

5. Click **Connect to Picture.**

➤ **To specify ringtones and sounds**

1. In the **Lync Options** dialog box, click the **Ringtones and Sounds** page.

2. Select the phone number you want to work with, and then select the ringtone you want to assign to the number.

3. Use the **Sounds** options to specify whether and when Lync plays sounds to notify you of events.

4. Click **Sound Settings** to open the **Sound** dialog box.

5. In the **Program Events** list, scroll to view the options for Microsoft Lync 2010.

6. Select the event you want to work with, and then select the sound file you want to associate with that event.

➤ **To change file saving paths**

1. Display the **File Saving** page of the **Lync Options** dialog box.

2. Click the **Browse** button for the setting you want to change.

3. In the **Browse for Folder** dialog box, select the new location and then click **OK.**

Practice Tasks

Practice the skills you learned in this section by performing the following tasks in Lync. If you are just learning how to work with Lync, you might want to return to the Lync Options dialog box after you gain more practice. To start, do the following:

- Sign in to Lync and then open the Options dialog box.
- Enter phone numbers you want to share with appropriate contacts.
- If you have a webcam, go to the Video Device page and update the settings for the webcam.
- Use the Ringtones And Sounds page to experiment with the audio clues Lync can provide.

3.2 Employ Collaboration Tools and Techniques

In this section, you'll explore the range of ways in which Lync enables collaboration, including group conversations in which you can review, annotate, or update documents; online meetings; instant messaging; and audio and video conferences.

Holding Group Conversations

During an online meeting or a call that you set up with Lync, you can supplement and focus the conversation by using Lync to share information. You can open a Microsoft PowerPoint presentation, for example, and discuss and annotate the presentation's slides. You can share your entire desktop or the content you are working on in a specific program. You can also use an online whiteboard to gather ideas in a brainstorming session or conduct a quick poll to collect opinions.

Later in this section, you'll learn more details about conferences and online meetings, but one quick way to initiate a group conversation is to click the arrow next to the Options button, click Meet Now, and then use the People Options button to invite one person or more to join a discussion with you. (You can also drag a contact entry from the Lync window to the conversation window to invite that person to a conversation.) With the group assembled online, you can then use commands on the conversation window's Share menu to collaborate in a number of ways.

Important The participants in a group conversation that you set up with the Meet Now command are designated as presenters by default. Presenters can share content and perform other operations during a conversation that participants designated as attendees cannot. When you invite participants by using the People Options button, choose Make Everyone An Attendee if you (as the organizer) want more control of the conversation.

Sharing Your Desktop

To work as a group on a document, to view a web page, or to review other content, you can share your desktop as part of a group conversation. You can grant control of your desktop to another participant (either a presenter or an attendee) and let that participant work with the programs or files on your computer. Participants can also request control, which you can approve or reject.

Tip Sharing your desktop through Lync can be a helpful way to troubleshoot or solve a problem you are having with your system. Start a conversation in Lync with a member of your help desk staff or a colleague who has experience in the area you're having trouble with. You can turn over control to that person so that he can check settings and configurations on your computer.

In the conversation window, select Desktop from the Share menu to start this process. If you initiate this action, you can click Preview in the Lync window notification bar to see what participants are looking at.

Across the top of your screen, you'll see a toolbar that indicates you are currently sharing your desktop. Lync notifies participants in the conversation that you have shared content, and they can then accept (or decline) to view the shared content. Lync loads and displays your desktop in a portion of the Lync window referred to as the *stage*.

Participants see activity on your desktop in real time. The text you type in a Word document, for example, appears on their screens as you type it. To turn over control to another participant, click Give Control and then select the participant from the list. If a participant clicks Request Control at the top of her screen, you see a notification that lets you accept or decline the request. You can regain control by clicking Give Control and choosing Take Back Control or by pressing Ctrl+Alt+Spacebar.

You work with the controls shown here when you share your desktop. You can grant access to another participant, say yes or no to a request sent to you, and take back control when you need to.

To avoid having to accept control requests from people you know, you can select Automatically Accept Control Requests, an option on the menu that appears when you click Give Control. Click Stop Sharing when you no longer need to share your desktop.

➤ **To share your desktop**

1. In the conversation window, click **Share** and then click **Desktop**.

2. In the notification bar, click **Preview** to see a small rendering of your desktop in the Lync stage.

3. To turn control over to a participant, click **Give Control** and then select the participant's name.

4. To regain control of your desktop, click **Give Control** and then select **Take Back Control**.

5. To close the shared desktop, click **Stop Sharing**.

Sharing a PowerPoint Presentation

When you select PowerPoint from the Share menu, Lync displays the Share PowerPoint dialog box, where you select the presentation you want to describe or talk through with others. Once Lync loads the presentation, you'll see the name of the presentation below the You Are Sharing label in the top-left corner of the stage. Participants in the conversation see a sharing request in Lync that they accept to see the presentation.

The tools at the bottom of the stage let you annotate a presentation (or a whiteboard). You can highlight text, add typewritten annotations, or work with a pen. Save the annotations when you finish.

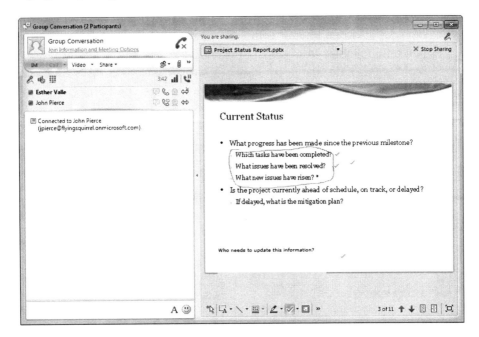

Although you can't add slides to a presentation you are sharing, the presentation isn't simply static content. You can add annotations, images, shapes, and other objects while you work in Lync to emphasize elements on a slide or to provide directions for modifications. The set of tools at the bottom of the stage area (from left to right) lets you do the following:

- **Point to objects**   Use the laser pointer if you are leading the conversation and want to point to a specific area or item on the current slide. A small ScreenTip appears in Lync to identify the participant who is pointing.

- **Select and type annotations**   Use this tool to type an annotation on the current slide. Click where you want the annotation to appear and then type. The text appears in a container you can select and drag to a different position if that's necessary. You can change the font and font size by clicking the down arrow at the right of this tool and then making the selections you want from the lists Lync displays.

- **Add lines and shapes**   The drawing tools let you add basic shapes to the slide—a plain line, a single arrow line, a double arrow line, an oval, and a rectangle. You can use these shapes to enclose text that needs modifications, for example, or to extend a line from an annotation to an object on the slide. Use the color selector just to the right of the drawing tools button to draw in a particular color. Participants can choose specific colors to identify their additions to the slide.

- **Write notes on the presentation using a pen or highlighter**   If you have a pen or stylus attached to your computer (or are adept at writing with a mouse), select a pen or highlighter from the options presented, and then add notes to the slide or highlight content that needs changes, further review, or different formatting, for example. You can choose from four colors for pens or highlighters, but you cannot change the line thickness.

- **Add check marks, arrows, and Xs**   Another way to annotate a slide is by using one of the stamp shapes available. You can add a check mark, an arrow, or an X. Use the arrow at the right of this tool to choose the stamp you want to add.

- **Insert images**   Click Insert Image to choose an image to add to the current slide. Use the handle at the bottom-right corner of the image to resize it. You can drag the image to change its position on the slide.

- **Save the presentation with the annotations you've added**   Click this button to create an XPS file of the presentation showing the annotations added during the group conversation.

> **Tip** You can view an XPS file in most web browsers or in a viewer application available from Microsoft.

Attendees as well as presenters can annotate the slides. Only presenters can save an annotated presentation. As the group reviews the presentation, a presenter can use the up and down arrows at the right of the presentation window to navigate back and forth between slides. Presenters (but not attendees) can also click the Thumbnails button to display thumbnail images of the slides along the right side of the stage. If you want to see the notes related to a slide, click Presenter Notes. Both of these buttons toggle on and off the display of these features.

> **Tip** You can display the presentation in full screen by clicking the Full Screen button in the bottom-right corner of the stage. Click Esc to show the presentation within the Lync application window again.

➤ **To share and annotate a presentation**

1. In the conversation window, click **Share** and then click **PowerPoint Presentation**.

2. In the **Share PowerPoint** dialog box, select the PowerPoint file you want to share.

3. Use the tools at the bottom of the stage to annotate the slides.

4. Click **Save with Annotations** to save the presentation with your annotations in place.

Sharing Content from the Stage

When you stop sharing content during a conversation, the content remains available if you need to refer to it again. Use the drop-down list at the top-left corner of the stage to view a record of the shared content. Click the arrow related to an item to open a menu that lets you share that content again, save it, rename it, and so on. Choose Share New Content to select a different program, presentation, or sharing option.

You can manage shared content using this menu in the stage.

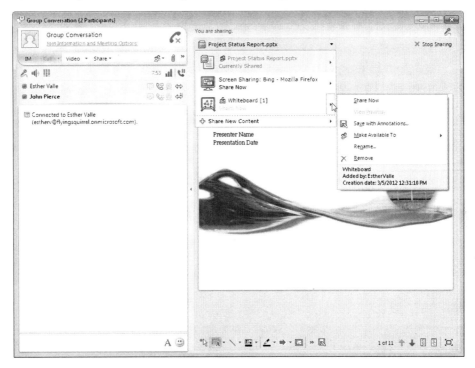

You can also add attachments to the conversation window during a meeting. Click Add Or View Attachments in the conversation window's toolbar, and then click Add Attachment. Choose the file or files you want to provide to participants. Participants then click in the notification area of their conversation window to view or save the attachments.

> **Tip** You can also drag a file into the conversation window to add it to a conversation. If you want to cancel the transfer of an attachment, press Alt+Q.

Sharing a Program

Sharing your desktop lets participants in a group conversation see everything that's currently running on your computer. If instead of sharing your desktop, you want to share a document in a particular program, start the program and then choose the Program command on the Share menu.

> **Important** The program you want to share must be running on your computer before you share it. In other words, Lync doesn't give you the option to start a program when you choose the Program command.

When you select Program, Lync displays the Share Programs dialog box, which shows thumbnail images of other programs currently running on your computer. Select the program or programs you want to share (hold down the Ctrl key to select more than one), and then click the Share button.

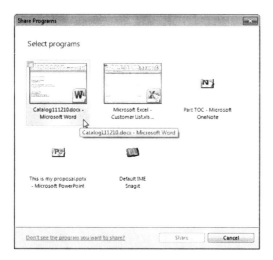

Instead of sharing your desktop, share one or more specific programs to work on documents as a group.

A shared program comes to the foreground on your computer and is displayed in the stage on participants' computers. You can give control of the program to a participant, who can then interact with the program. Use the Give Control button to select a participant, to choose the option to automatically accept control requests, and to take back control if you've released it. A participant can also request control.

> **Important** You cannot share the following programs: Lync 2010, Microsoft Lync 2010 Recording Manager, Microsoft Lync 2010 Attendee, Windows Explorer, Sticky Notes, Windows Sidebar, or any program running with user privileges that are higher than the privileges for Lync 2010.

➤ To share a program

1. In the conversation window, click **Share** and then click **Program**.

2. In the **Share Programs** dialog box, select the program or programs you want to share with participants.

3. Click **Share**.

4. Use the **Give Control** button to grant control to a participant if necessary.

5. Click **Stop Sharing** when the session is over.

Conducting an Online Poll

You can use a group conversation in Lync as a forum to conduct a simple opinion poll. The New Poll command on the Share menu opens the Create A Poll dialog box. Provide a name for the poll, type a question, and then enter the set of choices. You can provide up to seven options for users to choose from. When you click OK in this dialog box, the poll questions appear in the stage area.

Inform group decisions by the opinions collected in a poll conducted in Lync.

When you first post a poll, the poll is open but responses are hidden from attendees. Presenters can use the buttons at the bottom of the stage to close the poll, show results to all participants, edit the poll question and choices, and clear votes. When you choose to edit the poll question and answers, the current answers are cleared. Once the results are in, you can save the poll as a PNG image file or as a comma-separated value file (.csv) that you can open in Microsoft Excel.

> **Tip** To conduct a poll with multiple questions, define the first question, collect answers, and then save that poll. Then edit the current poll and define a new question and set of answers.

➤ **To create and manage a poll**

1. In the conversation window, click **Share** and then click **New Poll**.

2. In the **Create a Poll** dialog box, type a name for the poll, the question, and the array of possible answers.

3. Click **OK** to display the poll in the stage.

4. After participants have answered the poll question, close the poll, reveal the results to attendees, and edit the poll to provide a new question if needed.

5. Click **Save Poll** to preserve the results.

6. Click **Stop Sharing** to clear the stage.

Working Together on a Whiteboard

For a group brainstorming session, share a new whiteboard. Lync displays a blank page in the stage area and provides a set of tools at the bottom of the window that lets you sketch and outline your ideas. The tools available are essentially the same as those you can use to annotate a shared PowerPoint presentation. For a description of these tools, see "Sharing a PowerPoint Presentation" earlier in this chapter.

Take a look at the notification above the top-left corner of the stage that indicates that everyone in the group conversation can contribute to the whiteboard. With a white-board displayed, you won't see the Give Control or Request Control buttons. To preserve the working session you conduct with a whiteboard, save it. You can save a whiteboard as an XPS file or a PNG file.

➤ **To share a whiteboard**

1. In the conversation window, click **Share** and then click **New Whiteboard**.

2. Use the tools at the bottom of the stage to add ideas and sketches to the whiteboard.

3. Click the **Save with Annotations** button to preserve the whiteboard as an XPS or a PNG file.

Holding Web Conferences

If you set up your Office 365 e-mail account in Outlook 2010, you can schedule a meeting that is held online using Lync.

> **Tip** You can use the Mail option in Control Panel to set up your Office 365 e-mail account in Outlook 2010. In the Mail Setup dialog box, click E-Mail Accounts and then click New. Walk through the Add New Account wizard. After you enter your name, e-mail address, and password, your settings should be configured automatically. Be aware that in some organizations, this operation might be restricted.

Display the calendar in Outlook 2010, and then click New Online Meeting on the Calendar view's Home tab. Outlook opens a new meeting request and adds a link that you and recipients can use to start and join the meeting at the scheduled time. You can then address the meeting request to recipients, type the subject, and add other information.

You can set up online meetings in Outlook 2010. Click Join Online Meeting to open the Lync conversation window and conduct the meeting.

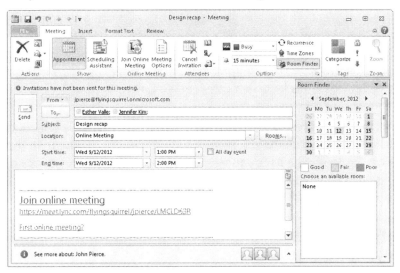

Before you send the meeting request, click Meeting Options in the Online Meeting group on the Meeting tab. Use the dialog box that's displayed to change options for access and presenters. By default, everyone you invite to an online meeting, including external contacts, can join the meeting without having to be admitted. Instead of admitting everyone, you can set up a meeting so that only the organizer is admitted immediately, only people from your organization, or only those people in your organization who you invite directly.

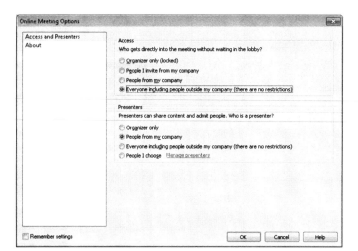

Manage an online meeting by setting options for who will be admitted automatically and who will be designated presenters.

For presenters, the default setting is that everyone from your company who attends the meeting is a presenter. You can choose instead Organizer Only, select the option that imposes no restrictions, or designate presenters. If you select People I Choose, click Manage Presenters to identify the individuals who can serve in that role. (You must have already added recipients to the meeting request to designate presenters. If you haven't done this, the list you see when you click Manage Presenters is blank.)

> **Tip** If you want to use these settings for other online meetings, select the option Remember Settings in the lower-left corner of the Online Meeting Options dialog box.

To start the meeting, open the meeting request and click Join Online Meeting on the Meeting tab or double-click the link in the meeting request. (If you open the meeting request in Outlook Web App, you need to click the link.) Those actions open the conversation window in Lync, with the meeting's subject line in the title bar. (If a meeting participant doesn't have Lync installed, she can join the meeting by using the Lync Attendee. When the participant clicks the Join Online Meeting link, the option to download Lync Attendee is provided, which lets the participant join the meeting without having the full Lync client.)

If meeting options were set up so that admittance to the meeting is not automatic, the organizer needs to admit attendees who are waiting. These attendees see a notification that they are waiting in the lobby.

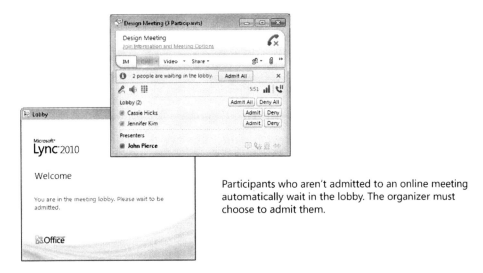

Participants who aren't admitted to an online meeting automatically wait in the lobby. The organizer must choose to admit them.

During a meeting, presenters can share content, and they can record an online meeting to capture audio and video, including discussions of shared content. To begin recording a meeting, click the More Options arrow at the right side of the conversation window toolbar and choose Start Recording. Use the same menu to pause recording and to stop recording.

When you stop a recording, Lync displays a dialog box in which you can specify a recording title (the meeting subject is used by default) and also choose to create a version of the recording that you can publish for others to see. The path in the Save To box shows the default location or a different location specified in the Lync Options dialog box.

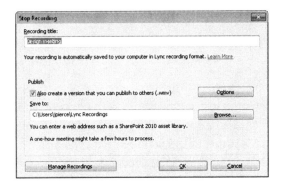

If you want to share a recording with other users, keep the option to create a version that you can publish.

See Also For more information about working with recorded meetings, see "Using Recording Manager" later in this chapter.

Participants can leave a meeting by clicking the phone icon at the top right of the conversation window. The meeting's organizer can end a meeting by clicking the People Options button and then choosing Remove Everyone And End Meeting.

➤ **To schedule an online meeting**

1. Open Outlook 2010, and switch to **Calendar** view.
2. On the **Home** tab, click **New Online Meeting**.
3. Add the meeting attendees, type a subject, and then add any message to the body of the meeting request.
4. In the meeting request, click **Meeting Options** if you need to change default settings for meeting access and the designation of presenters.
5. Click **Send**.

➤ **To join an online meeting**

1. Open the meeting request.
2. Click the link embedded in the request.

   Lync opens the conversation window. You might need to specify how you want to join the audio portion of the meeting.

➤ **To record a meeting**

1. In the conversation window, click the **More Options** arrow at the right side of the toolbar.
2. Click **Start Recording**.
3. Click **Pause Recording** if necessary during the meeting.
4. Click **Stop Recording** when you are ready.

Sending Instant Messages

You will frequently use Lync to exchange instant messages with contacts and coworkers. You only need to double-click the contact's entry in the Lync window or right-click the entry and choose Send An Instant Message. In the window that Lync displays, type your message and then press Enter. The message's recipient receives a notification of the message from Lync and can reply with a return message, redirect the message as a Lync call, ignore the message, or indicate that he doesn't want to be disturbed.

You can engage in more than one instant message conversation at the same time. After you start the first instant message session, right-click another contact and send an instant message to that person as well. You can also add multiple contacts to a single instant message session. Select the first contact, press the Ctrl key, and then select the other contacts you want to include.

> **Tip** You can send an instant message to a group of contacts by right-clicking the group's name in the contact list and choosing Send An Instant Message. You can add a contact to an instant message session by dragging the contact's entry from the contact list in the Lync window to the conversation window.

In most respects, an instant message session is like other group conversations you hold in Lync. You can share your desktop or a presentation, for example, or set up a poll or a whiteboard. While an instant message session is under way, you can copy and paste text and links to websites or documents into the instant message window. To add another contact to the conversation, click the People Options button and then invite that person to join via e-mail, by searching your contact list, or by dragging the contact's entry into the conversation window. You can use other options on this menu to make all other participants attendees (which means they can't share content) or to end the session.

During the conversation, use the Share menu to open a presentation, share your desktop or a program, or open a whiteboard for brainstorming. To add a video feed, click Video and then click Start A Video Call. If you want to switch from exchanging instant messages to a Lync call, click Call to set up a conference call with the people in the session. The other participants are notified of the switch and need to join the call to become active in it.

The formatting buttons at the bottom of the instant message window let you emphasize text, change the font, and add emoticons.

Use the formatting button at the bottom of the conversation window to change to a different font or to apply formatting such as bold or italic. Click Select An Emoticon to display a palette of icons you can add to a message for emphasis and humor.

Responding to an E-mail Message or a Call with an Instant Message

When a contact calls you in Lync or sends you an e-mail message, you can respond with an instant message instead.

For a call, click the Redirect button on the notification Lync displays when you receive the call, and then choose Reply With Instant Message. When you choose this command, Lync opens the instant message window and the person who calls is informed that you chose to reply in that way. Lync also informs the caller that you've invited her to a conversation. Type your reply in the instant message window and then press Enter to continue.

For an e-mail message you receive in Outlook Web App, you can respond with an instant message by right-clicking the contact's name in the reading pane and choosing Chat. You can also open the message and then click Chat in the toolbar. In Outlook 2010, you can double-click a contact's name to display a small contact card. In the toolbar at the top of the contact card, click the Send An Instant Message To button.

Sending a File in an Instant Message

You can send file attachments in an instant message. The recipient of the message can then choose to accept the file, save it, or decline its delivery. The recipient can also double-click the notification Lync displays to open the file. By default, files that are accepted, saved, or transferred are stored in the My Received Files folder in the user's Documents library.

The sender of the instant message sees a message indicating the action taken by the recipient.

Add to the content of an instant message session by including an attachment. By default, attachments are saved in a user's Documents library, in the folder My Received Files.

➤ **To send an instant message to a contact**

1. Right-click the contact's entry, and then choose **Send an Instant Message**.

2. Type your message in the conversation window, and then press Enter.

3. Use the formatting tools at the bottom of the conversation to change fonts, to add bold or italic emphasis, or to insert an emoticon in the instant message.

> **To redirect an instant message to a Lync call**

➜ In the instant message notification you receive, click **Redirect** and then choose **Respond with Lync Call**.

> **To reply to an e-mail message with an instant message**

➜ In Outlook Web App, open the e-mail message and then click **Chat**.

Audio Conferencing

Lync calls use Voice over Internet Protocol (VoIP) for communication between computers. When you place a call to a contact, each device that the contact has enabled to receive calls from Lync rings—which might include a desktop computer as well as a laptop. Calls you place via Lync bypass the standard telephone network.

Start a Lync call by pointing at a contact and then clicking Call. During the call, you can add contacts by pointing to the People Options button and then inviting other people to join the conference.

You can start a group call by selecting each contact you want to talk to. (Use the Ctrl key to select more than one entry in the contact list.) Right-click the selection, and then choose Start A Conference Call.

> **To start a conference call with multiple contacts**

1. Select the contacts you want to call.
2. Right-click the selection, and then choose **Start a Conference Call**.

Setting Up a Video Conference

If you have a webcam connected to your computer, you can include a video feed in the group conversations you hold in Lync.

After you connect the webcam, go to the Lync Options dialog box and check the settings for focus, brightness, and other properties. (See "Video Device Page" earlier in this chapter for more details.) You can then select a contact (or a group of contacts), right-click, and choose Start A Video Call.

You see your own video feed in a preview window that is inset at the bottom-right corner of the conversation window. The Video menu includes a command that lets you hide the preview or expand it so that it's shown in a larger portion of the conversation window. Use the Video menu also to end or pause your video stream, to view the video in full screen, and to display the video feed in its own window. (The standalone video window includes a button in its top-right corner that lets you incorporate the video in the conversation window again.)

As you can in conversations that don't feature video, use the Share menu to display your desktop, a specific program, a whiteboard, and other such items to the participants in the video call. Click the IM button in the conversation window to send a participant an instant message during the call.

When you click End Video, the call itself is not ended. You can carry on via voice or instant messaging.

If you are engaged in a group conversation, open the Video menu and then choose Add Video to start a video feed for the conversation.

➤ **To set up a video call**

1. Select the contact or contacts you want to include in the video call.

2. Right-click the selection, and then choose **Start Video Call**.

3. During the call, use the **Video** menu to do the following:

   - Hide, show, expand, or shrink your preview
   - Pause the video
   - View the video in full screen
   - View the video in a separate window
   - End the video

Practice Tasks

Practice the skills you learned in this section by performing the following tasks in Lync:

- Work with colleagues in your organization to hold a group conversation. If you organize the conversation, share your desktop or a presentation with the other participants.

- Exchange instant messages with your colleagues. Redirect an instant message to a Lync call.

- If you and your colleagues have webcams available, set up and conduct a video conference.

3.3 Manage Lync Contacts

In many ways, your contact list is the center of your work in Lync. Using the list, you can initiate calls, send instant messages or e-mail, schedule a meeting, and perform other tasks. You learned how many of these features work in the previous section. In this section, you'll learn more about organizing and managing your contacts in Lync.

Using Contact Groups

Organizing Lync contacts into groups helps you find a contact and, more important, lets you communicate with all the members of the group in one step. Lync sets up two groups by default: Frequent Contacts and Other Contacts. You can create your own groups and then add contacts to them.

> **Tip** You can also create a group when you add a contact to your list. You'll learn how to do this in the next section.

After you add contacts to a group, point to the group's name in the contact list to display the Call button. Click Call to start a conference call with the group's members. For more options, right-click a group name to display a menu from which you can do the following:

- Send an instant message to the group
- Start a conference call
- Start a video call
- Share your desktop in a group conversation
- Send an e-mail message to group members
- Schedule a meeting with group members (if your account uses Outlook 2010)

➤ **To create a group**

1. Above the contacts list, click **Groups**.
2. In the list, right-click a group name (for example, **Other Contacts**) and choose **Create New Group**.
3. Type a name for the group, and then click away from the text box.

➤ **To communicate with group members**

1. Right-click the group name.
2. On the menu, choose the command for how you want to communicate with the group. For example, choose **Send an Instant Message** or **Start a Video Call**.

Finding and Adding Contacts

Use the search box in the Lync window to locate a contact you want to add to your list or communicate with. Lync can search by name, e-mail address, or phone number. Lync lists the contact or makes suggestions on the basis of the characters you type. Point to the contact you want to add (if more than one is displayed), and then click the plus sign to open a menu that lets you pin the contact to your group of frequent contacts or add the contact to the Other Contacts group, a group you defined, or a new group.

Lync locates contacts after you type just a few characters. Add contacts to a built-in group, a group you define, or a new group.

If you simply want to communicate with one of the contacts Lync found, click Call or right-click the contact's entry and then choose Send An Instant Message, Share, or another of the available commands.

When you add a contact to your list, the person you add is notified of the action and can choose to add you to a specific contact group and to select the privacy relationship that she wants to apply. You can ignore the notification or click Remind Me Later to postpone making the settings you want for this contact.

Lync notifies a contact that you've added to your list. He or she can then specify a contact group and apply a privacy relationship.

➤ To find and add a contact

1. In the search box, start typing the name, e-mail address, or phone number for a contact you are looking for.

2. In the list Lync displays, point to the contact you want to add.

3. Click the plus sign, and then select the group you want to add the contact to or select **Add to New Group**.

4. If you select **Add to New Group**, type the group name in the text box Lync provides.

Editing and Managing Contact Groups

When you right-click a group name in the contacts list, you can use commands on that menu to do the following:

- Move a group up or down in the contact list.
- Rename a group.
- Delete the group.
- View a contact card for the group. From the group contact card, you can send an e-mail or an instant message to the group, start a conference call or a video call, or share your desktop in a group conversation.

➤ To edit and manage contact groups

→ In the contact list, right-click a contact group and then choose one of the following commands:
  - ○ Move Group Up
  - ○ Move Group Down
  - ○ Rename Group
  - ○ Delete Group
  - ○ View Contact Card

Specifying Contact Relationships

One way in which you manage the information that Lync provides about your status, schedule, availability, and activities is by specifying the relationship you have with a contact. Depending on the category you place a contact in, that contact can see more or less of your contact information and activities. You can add a contact to the following categories:

- Friends And Family
- Workgroup
- Colleagues
- External Contacts
- Blocked Contacts

Contacts in your organization are designated as colleagues by default. You can change the relationship for a contact by right-clicking the contact's entry and choosing Change Privacy Relationship.

Privacy relationships determine what information a contact can see. Coworkers are designated colleagues by default. Choose Blocked Contacts to reveal no information to someone.

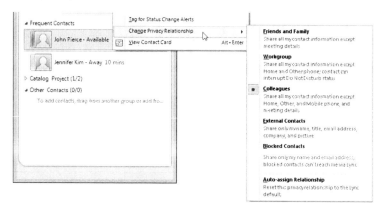

The following table, taken from the Lync Help content, lists the information available within each relationship.

> **Note** An asterisk (*) indicates that if this attribute is defined in the company's directory service, it will be visible to all contacts in your organization, regardless of the privacy relationship, and to external contacts (if configured and recognized by your organization's network). A pound sign (#) indicates that this attribute is visible by default.

Presence Information	External Contacts	Colleagues	Workgroup	Friends And Family
Presence Status	X	X	X	X
Display Name	X	X	X	X
Email Address	X	X	X	X
Title*	X	X	X	X
Work Phone*		X	X	X
Mobile Phone*			X	X
Home Phone*				X
Other Phone				X
Company*	X	X	X	X
Office*	X	X	X	X
Work Address*	X	X	X	X
SharePoint Site*	X	X	X	X
Meeting Location#			X	
Meeting Subject#			X	
Free Busy		X	X	X
Working Hours		X	X	X
Location#		X	X	X
Notes (Out-of-Office Note)		X	X	X
Notes (Personal)		X	X	X
Last Active		X	X	X
Personal Photo Web Address	X	X	X	X

➤ **To specify a privacy relationship**

1. Right-click the entry for the contact you want to work with.
2. Point to **Change Privacy Relationship** and then select the setting you want to apply to this contact.

Managing Status and Presence Settings

Your current status appears under your name in the Lync window. By default, Lync uses entries in your Outlook calendar to set your status. For example, during the time period for an appointment, your status shows that you are busy. When you are engaged in a call, Lync changes your status to In A Call. Likewise, Lync uses the status settings In A Meeting and In A Conference Call when you are involved in those activities.

You can also manually change your status to alert your contacts that you are away or don't want to be disturbed. The choices for your status are as follows:

- **Available**   Your status is set to Available when Lync detects you're using your computer. You can set your status to Available yourself as well.

- **Busy**   Lync sets your status to Busy when you have an appointment on your calendar in Outlook. You can also set your status to Busy manually.

- **Do Not Disturb**   You can select this status from the menu of options. When your status is set to Do Not Disturb, you don't see any instant messages or calls, but you will see any calls or instant messages you missed in the conversation history in Outlook.

- **Be Right Back**   This is another status setting that you set yourself.

- **Off Work**   You select this status when you are away from your office and from work.

- **Appear Away**   Set your status to Appear Away when you don't want to be contacted.

> **Tip** To revert from the status you set and have Lync automatically update your status, click Reset Status.

Lync sets your status as Inactive and then Away after your computer is idle for the period of time specified in the Lync Options dialog box. For more information, see "Status Page" earlier in this chapter.

You will also see status settings such as Offline or Unknown for your contacts. Lync sets your status to Offline when you log off your computer. The Unknown status setting is shown when Lync can't detect the status of a contact.

The presence states defined in Lync can't be customized, and you can't create presence states of your own. However, if you want to give your contacts more details about where you are or what you're doing, add a note in the text box above your name (which displays the prompt "What's happening today?"). The note you add here appears with your contact card and in the Activity Feeds lists for your contacts. You can also add a place to the Set Your Location box (Home and Work are suggested by Lync) to associate a location with the network you are connected to.

➤ To set your presence status

1. Click the arrow next to the current status setting, and then select the setting you want.

2. To reset your status so that Lync sets it automatically based on your activity, choose **Reset Status from the options on this menu**.

Managing Activity Feeds

You can let your contacts know more about what you're up to by typing a note in the text box above your name. The notes you add are displayed under your entry in the contacts list as well as in the Activity Feeds list. In addition to the notes you add, the Activity Feeds list shows status changes, changed pictures, and updated contact information.

As you can with conversations and calls, you can view and filter activity feeds. Above the search box, click the Activity Feeds button (the middle one) to display the current list. Use the filters at the top of the list to view all activities for your contacts, the activities of only your frequent contacts, or the activities you entered for yourself. The entries in the Activity Feeds list act like regular contact entries. You can double-click an entry to send that contact an instant message, for example. Right-click the entry to see other options.

> **Tip** By default, updates to your personal note appear in the Activity Feeds list for everyone (except blocked contacts and external contacts). To not show notes, open the Lync Options dialog box and clear the Show All My Updates In Activity Feed option on the Personal page.

➤ **To manage activity feeds**

1. Above the contacts list, click the **Activities Feed** button.
2. Use the filters to see all activity feeds, the activities of your frequent contacts, or your own activities.

Viewing Conversation History

Lync can maintain a history of the calls and conversations you have with contacts. You can look back on this information to see calls you missed or to pick up a conversation you want to continue. You can also view recent conversations you had with particular contacts.

The View Conversation History command appears on the File menu. (The command might not be available. Its availability depends on how Lync 2010 is set up in your organization.)

When you choose this command, Microsoft Outlook runs, and you see your recent incoming and outgoing instant messages, phone calls, and meetings listed in the Conversation History folder.

If you want to see the entries for a particular contact in Outlook, right-click the contact in Lync and then choose Find Previous Conversations.

You can also see a record of your conversations in Lync. Above the search box, click the Conversations button. Lync displays a list of phone calls, missed calls (if any), meetings, instant message sessions, and group conversations. Use the filters at the top of the list to see all conversations, just missed calls, or calls (including group conversations, missed calls, and online meetings). Here is an explanation of the options you see:

- All shows your 100 most-recent conversations.

- Missed shows any missed conversation during that timeframe (up to the 100 most recent).

- Calls shows any calls during that timeframe (up to the 100 most recent).

Filter the conversation history list in Lync to find recent conversations and calls and to continue a conversation when necessary.

To continue a call, for example, point to an entry in the conversation list and then click Rejoin. For an instant message session, double-click the entry to open the conversation window with the previous conversation intact. You can also point to an instant message session and then click Call.

To delete a conversation from the list, right-click the entry and choose Delete Conversation. You can also use this menu to continue a conversation.

➤ **To view the Conversation History folder**

→ On the **File** menu, click **View Conversation History**.

Microsoft Outlook opens and displays the Conversation History folder. You can then sort conversations or search for a conversation by keyword or contact.

➤ **To find a previous conversation with a specific contact**

→ In the contacts list, right-click the contact, and then choose **Find Previous Conversations**.

Outlook opens and displays that contact's conversations in the Conversation History folder.

➤ **To find and manage a recent or missed conversation**

1. Above the search box, click the **Conversations** icon.

2. Use the filters to see all or a subset of the conversations.

3. Point to an entry for a conversation you want to continue, and then click **Rejoin** or **Call**.

4. Right-click the conversation entry you want to remove, and then click **Delete Conversation**.

5. If the conversation you are looking for is not among your most recent 100 conversations, click **View More in Outlook** to open the **Outlook Conversation History** folder.

Practice Tasks

Practice the skills you learned in this section by performing the following tasks in Lync:

- Set up contact groups for projects you are working on currently. Add members of the project teams as contacts.

- Add a personal note and then view the note in the Activity Feeds list.

- Start calls, meetings, and other activities, and observe how Lync automatically changes your status.

3.4 Use Lync Tools

This section describes features in Lync that you use to manage recordings, take notes during a conversation, redirect a conversation, and handle a series of incoming calls.

Using Recording Manager

The Lync Recording Manager is a separate application. You can open it directly from the Start menu (Lync doesn't need to be running) or from the Tools menu in the Lync application window when you are signed in to Lync.

> **Tip** When you stop recording a conversation or a meeting, you'll see a notification that the recording is available. You can also open Recording Manager by clicking the notification.

In Recording Manager, you can replay recordings, browse to the location where a recording is stored, and delete a recording. If you are working with Lync recordings (as opposed to Windows Media recordings), you can rename a recording or save all or parts of the recording in Windows Media format and publish it for other people to view.

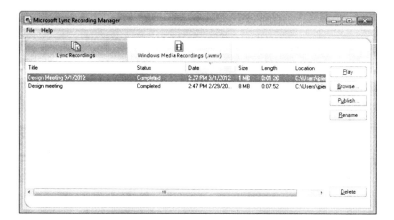

The Recording Manager lets you replay recordings and publish recordings for other users.

When you use the Recording Manager to replay a recording (select a recording and click Play or double-click the recording to start it), you view the recording in the Lync Recording Player. In this window, you hear the audio and watch the video (if any) of the meeting and can also see what content was being shared. Use the Information And Attachments button at the top of the Recording Player window to see a list of participants and attachments (if any) that were included in the meeting. When you click Content Sharing And People Speaking, you display or hide a pane that shows which content was shared during the meeting and who is speaking. The Recording Player also lets you show or hide a meeting's video feed. Use the controls at the bottom of the window to stop or pause the recording and adjust the volume.

On the Lync Recordings tab, you have the additional options of renaming a recording and publishing it to a public location (such as a SharePoint site). To make a recording publicly available, click Publish on the Lync Recordings tab. In the Save And Publish dialog box, use the Browse button to navigate to the location where you'll publish the recording. Click the Options button to specify which types of content to include in the published version. For example, if you want to reduce the size of the file you are publishing, clear the Participant Video option in the Save And Publish Options dialog box because video can take up a lot of space and might not be of good quality. You can also use the Save And Publish Options dialog box to specify start and end times for parts of the recording you want to publish.

Set the Start Time and End Time to publish a segment of a recording. Clear the Participant Video option to reduce the file size for the recording.

➤ **To manage recordings**

1. On the **Start** menu, click **All Programs**, **Microsoft Lync**, **Microsoft Lync Recording Manager**. (You can also start the Recording Manager by selecting Recording Manager from the Tools menu in Lync.)

2. Select a recording you want to view, and then click **Play**.

3. To make a recording available to others, on the **Lync Recordings** tab, select a recording and then click **Publish**.

4. In the **Save and Publish** dialog box, type a name for the shared recording.

5. Click **Browse** to open the location where you want to post the recording.

6. Click **Options**, and then in the **Save and Publish Options** dialog box, select which content to include in the recording and specify start and end times if you don't want to publish the entire recording.

7. Click **OK** to save your selections and close the dialog boxes.

Using the Always On Top Option

To keep the Lync window visible so that it is on top of other windows, choose Always On Top from the Tools menu. The Lync window is small enough that you can position it in a corner of your screen and continue working in other applications. Clear this setting when you want the Lync window to move to the background when another application is active.

➤ **To keep the Lync window on top**

1. Click the arrow next to the **Options** button.
2. Point to **Tools**, and then choose **Always On Top**.

Taking Notes in OneNote

If you don't want to make a recording of a meeting, you can take notes in Microsoft OneNote while the conversation takes place and then compile and distribute notes to participants.

Start a conversation or an online meeting and then click the More Options arrow at the right end of the conversation window's toolbar. Then choose Take Notes Using OneNote, which starts OneNote and adds a page to the Unfiled Notes area. In OneNote, you can move this page to a specific notebook (a notebook for a specific project, for example) after you conclude the conversation.

The page OneNote displays is tentatively titled Conversation and includes the date and a time stamp of when the conversation began. The page also lists the participants. To take notes, just start typing on the page, in the note container that OneNote provides. You can add notes to a different area of the page by clicking and then typing the text.

Taking notes in OneNote is not the same as sharing a program through Lync. If you start OneNote, you are the only conversation participant working in that instance of the program.

> **See Also** If you aren't familiar with Microsoft OneNote, it is a notebook application that comes with some editions of Microsoft Office 2010. You can find out more at *www.microsoft.com/office/onenote*.

Ending the conversation in Lync doesn't close OneNote. Keep OneNote open if you want to edit and organize the raw notes, move the page to a notebook, insert images or files to augment the notes you've taken, and so on. You don't need to save your work in OneNote—the program saves new content automatically. Close OneNote when you're ready.

➤ **To take notes in OneNote**

1. Start a group conversation, instant message session, or an online meeting.

2. In the conversation window, click the **More Options** button and then choose **Take Notes in OneNote**.

3. Add notes (typewritten or handwritten) to the new page in OneNote.

4. When the conversation concludes, edit the notes in OneNote. You can distribute them as an attachment in Lync or post them to a shared location, if necessary.

Changing the Conversation Subject

When you initiate a Lync call or an instant message exchange, you can specify a conversation topic so that the person you are contacting knows what you want to talk about. The subject you enter appears in the notification that Lync displays for the contact or contacts you call.

During the conversation, you can change the subject when you need to. For example, you might update the subject when you are working through a meeting agenda. The subject you enter in Lync appears in the title bar in the conversation window.

The Change Conversation Subject command is on the More Options menu. Choose this command and then type the subject you want to use.

➤ **To change the conversation subject**

1. In the conversation window, click the **More Options** button at the right end of the toolbar.

2. Choose **Change Conversation Subject**.

3. Type the subject in the dialog box Lync displays, and then click **OK**.

Practice Tasks

Practice the skills you learned in this section by performing the following tasks on your site:

- Set up and record a meeting with some of your coworkers.
- Use the Recording Manager to publish an excerpt of the recording.
- During the meeting, open OneNote and take notes about the conversation.
- Ask one or more of your colleagues to change the subject as you talk with each other.

Objective Review

Before finishing this chapter, be sure you have mastered the following skills:

3.1   Configure Lync options

3.2   Employ collaboration tools and techniques

3.3   Manage Lync contacts

3.4   Use Lync tools

4 Managing Sites in SharePoint Online

The skills tested in this section of the Microsoft Office exam for Office 365 relate to how you work in the SharePoint Online team site. Specifically, the following objectives are associated with this set of skills:

4.1 Search for site content

4.2 Manage sites

4.3 Manage content

The components of a SharePoint team site involve a broad range of operations, including searches, content management, approval workflows, team discussion boards, and assigning tasks. To support and perform these operations, you work with the Site Actions menu, a variety of commands on the SharePoint ribbon, and other controls, and you need an understanding of the work involved in managing the team site—the options you have to create document versions, for example, or which type of list you should use for a specific purpose. In this chapter, you'll begin by learning how to search for content on a SharePoint site. You'll then learn the details of managing sites and the content you store in SharePoint.

> **See Also** You can learn more about SharePoint from a number of sources, including the e-book *MOS 2010 Study Guide for Microsoft Office SharePoint*, available at *http://shop.oreilly.com/product/0790145336491.do.*

> **Important** Site permissions affect what a user can and cannot do in a SharePoint site. If you are not an Office 365 administrator or have not been assigned the Full Control permission for the team site, you might not be able to perform all the tasks described in this chapter.

4.1 Search for Site Content

As a repository of content that pertains to a project, your department, or another aspect of an organization's business, your team site contains many documents, list items, announcements, and other information. You can use links on the Quick Launch to open lists and libraries that you know hold the item you need. To find content when you aren't sure of its location or to find related content (all content by a specific author, for example), you can use the search box that appears at the top of the team site's home page and on list and library pages. You can refine and expand your search by using features such as advanced search or by filtering the search results.

You can search for content using keywords, a value such as a document author's name or a file name, or a particular phrase that you enclose in quotation marks. You can also search using a query syntax. For example, typing **Author:John AND filetype:docx** in the search box finds Word documents written by John. Typing **Author:John OR Author:Sam** returns items whose author is John and items whose author is Sam. Queries are not case sensitive.

> **See Also** For more information about the operators and logic you can use to create search queries, see the SharePoint Help topic "Write Effective Queries."

Setting a Search Scope

By default, SharePoint uses context to set the search scope. As the prompt in the search box on the home page indicates, when you run a search from that page, SharePoint looks for content across the site. If you run a search from a list or library, the scope is set to that list or library, and the search results include only matching items in that list or library.

Change Search Settings

If you have permission to change site settings, you can choose an option that lets users specify a search scope before a search is conducted. Choose Site Settings from the Site Actions menu, and then click Search Settings under Site Collection Administration. On the Search Settings page, in the Specify The Dropdown Mode For Search Boxes list, select Show Scopes Dropdown. After you click OK and return to the home page (or a list or library), you should see a drop-down menu to the left of the search box. (Refresh the page if you don't see the menu.) Choose a search scope from the options provided in the menu to set the scope before you run a search.

In addition to search scopes such as This List and This Site, you can use a menu on the search results page to rerun your search within a different scope. You'll see two additional options on this menu:

- **All Sites**   If you choose All Sites, SharePoint expands the search to include other sites within the current site collection.

> **Tip** You can also click the All Sites link in the notification below the search box.

- **People**   If you choose People, the results page includes links with which you can open a person's My Site, send an e-mail message, view the person on the organizational chart, and so on. Setting the search scope to People doesn't always apply. You would not use this option when you are searching for a specific word or phrase in the site's content.

> **See Also** For more information about the My Site feature, see "Working with Your My Site Profile" later in this chapter.

➤ **To set the search scope**

1. In the search box, type the phrase (enclose it in quotation marks to search on the precise phrase), keyword, or query you want to search for.

2. Click the search button to display the search results page.

3. On the search results page, select the search scope you want from the menu beside the search box.

4. Click the search button to see the new results.

Using Advanced Search

When you need to define criteria for more complex searches, use the advanced search box. In advanced search, you can work with fields that are set up to combine terms using operators such as AND and OR. You can also specify that the search results should include only a specific type of document. By combining advanced search criteria, you can, for example, search for Microsoft Excel documents in English that contain the phrase "Overhead projections" whose author is Sam Smith and that were modified later than last week.

In an advanced search, combine criteria such as search terms and properties to find specific content.

Tip Keep in mind that combining many criteria in an advanced search can affect the speed at which SharePoint returns results.

Set up an advanced search by using the following options and fields:

- **All Of These Words** The search results will contain items that include each word you specify. For example, to find documents written by Samantha Smith about the companies Contoso and Adventures Works, type **Smith Contoso Adventure Works**. The logic of this search parameter assumes that you included the AND operator, so the search phrase SharePoint uses behind the scenes to return results is Smith AND Contoso AND Adventure Works.

- **The Exact Phrase** The search results will contain items that include the phrase you enter. The phrase is not case sensitive.

- **Any Of These Words** The search results will contain items that contain any of words you enter. In other words, in conducting the search, SharePoint combines the terms with OR—for example, Budget OR Proposal—and the results it returns match this logic.

- **None Of These Words** The search results will contain items that do not contain the word or words you enter.

- Use the Language area to search for items in the language you specify. The options are English, French, German, Japanese, Simplified Chinese, and Traditional Chinese.

- In the Result Type area, select the type of document to include in your results. The options are All Results, Documents, Word Documents, Excel Documents, and

PowerPoint Presentations. Selecting a specific document type returns results that match multiple file extensions associated with that type of document. For example, choosing Word Documents returns files with the .doc, the .docx, and other file extensions related to Word.

- In the Property Restrictions section, specify a property you want to use as the basis of a search. For example, Author, Description, Name, Size, URL, Last Modified Date, Created By, and Last Modified By. Use the second list in this area to specify a condition. For the Author property, for example, you can choose Contains, Does Not Contain, Equals, or Does Not Equal. For Last Modified Date, choose either Equals, Later Than, or Earlier Than. Add additional properties to the search by clicking the plus sign.

➤ **To set up an advanced search**

1. On the search results page, click **Advanced**.

2. In the advanced search box, use the text boxes to define and combine the terms you want to search for. You can search for all words you enter, an exact phrase, any of the words you enter, or none of the words you use.

3. Select a language for the search results.

4. In the **Result Type** list, choose an option for the type of document you want to see.

5. Under **Add Property Restrictions**, use the lists and text boxes to define search criteria by choosing a property, specifying a condition, and typing a value. Use the plus sign to add criteria.

6. **Click Search**.

Working with Search Results

Along the left side of the search results page, SharePoint displays the refinement panel. By using this panel, you can tailor the search results to see items by a particular author, for example, or to see only Excel files. SharePoint provides categories such as the following:

- Result Type
- Site
- Author
- Modified Date
- Tags

Within each category, you can click one of the links listed to apply a filter. For example, under Result Type, click Word to show only Microsoft Word documents. Under Modified Date, click Past Week or Past Month to see results related to that time period. To return to the initial results, click the Any link (for example, Any Modified Date) at the top of the category you worked with.

➤ **To work in the refinement panel**

1. In the search box, type the phrase (enclosed in quotation marks), keyword, or query you want to search for.

2. Click the search button to display the **Search Results** page.

3. In the refinement panel, select a link under one of the categories provided to filter the search results.

Practice Tasks

Practice the skills you learned in this section by performing the following tasks on your site:

- If your team site does not contain content yet, create lists and libraries (see the procedures for doing this in the next section if needed) and upload documents and create list items you can search.

- Open one of the libraries, and use the search box to search for a phrase in one of the documents.

- Change the search scope to This Site, and run the search again to see whether other results appear.

- Use the advanced search box to search for a combination of words.

- Use the refinement panel to filter the search results by result type.

4.2 Manage Sites

In the following sections, you'll learn about features in SharePoint Online that you use to manage sites, including your My Site Profile, site permissions, and list and site templates.

Using Tags and Notes

Tags and notes are among the features SharePoint includes to promote and facilitate collaboration within a site. When a user adds a note or a tag to content such as a site page or a document, the content is classified with that tag. The site's users can then use the tag or note to find that document or page as well as related content. In addition to documents and site pages, users can add notes and tags to list items, libraries, and web pages outside the site.

> **Tip** My Site, which you learn about in the next section, includes features such as the activity feed and the tag cloud. These features help highlight information captured by tags and notes.

Adding a Note

The note board lets users record comments about an item in the context of a list or library. For example, a user can add a note about a web page while viewing the page. Other users can see the note and a link to the web page. Notes can be used on items such as a page, a document, or an external site. When notes are created, they appear in the note board that's associated with the list, library, or content and under the user's profile in the user's My Site. The ScreenTip that appears when you point to the Tags & Notes button indicates the number of notes that have been entered for a list, library, or page, for example.

You can also edit or update a note, and you can review notes made by colleagues by clicking the View Related Activities link displayed in the Tags And Notes section of a user's profile on My Site.

➤ To add a note

1. Open the document library or list to which you want to add a note.
2. Select a list item or document you want to add a note to.
3. On the ribbon, in the **Tag and Notes** section, click the **Tags & Notes** button to display the **Tags and Notes** dialog box.

   If you are adding a note for a library or list, the Tags & Notes button appears at the right side of the SharePoint window.
4. Click on the **Note Board** tab.
5. In the text box, type the note you want to make about the item, list, or library and then click **Post**.

Adding a Tag

A *tag* is a term that you want to assign to content. For example, you might create the following three tags for a document titled "Landscape Proposal for Contoso": "proposal," "landscape," and "Contoso." You might also use tags that identify who created the proposal and your contact at Contoso. Assigning a tag lets people locate documents more easily and improves searches when you use common terms. (Terms are stored in a central location so that they can be reused.) As you type a tag, SharePoint might suggest a term, and when you save tags, a list of suggested tags appears at the bottom of the Tags tab. Click one of these suggested tags to display a page that shows links to the content tagged with that term.

To classify content, assign a tag to documents, list items, libraries, and web pages. Use the links under Suggested Tags to see related site content.

Beside the Tags & Notes button, SharePoint displays the I Like It button. Click the button to apply the I Like It tag to pages, documents, and other content directly from the ribbon.

Tags are listed and displayed in the tag cloud in the Tags And Notes category of a user's profile on My Site. When you view the profile, you can click a tag to see a list of the documents and other items to which that user applied the tag.

➤ To add a tag

1. Open the library or list where you want to add a tag.
2. Select an item that you want to tag.
3. On the ribbon, in the **Tag and Notes** section, click the **Tags & Notes** button.
4. Click on the **Tags** tab, and then use the **Tags** text box to add tags you want to assign. Separate multiple terms by using a semicolon (;).
5. Click **Save**.

Working with Your My Site Profile

In addition to the team site, you can use your personal site (called *My Site*) to manage information in SharePoint Online. Click your user name in the top-right corner and then choose My Site to view your personal site's home page, or choose My Profile to view your profile and update information you want others to see.

A My Site profile offers several categories: Overview, Organization, Content, Notes and Tags, Colleagues, and Memberships. You use these categories to provide information about yourself, create relationships with colleagues and coworkers, and store personal and shared files. You can view the profiles of other people in your organization to find out what you might have in common with them. Your My Site profile is one of the ways in which SharePoint connects people.

> **Tip** Some of the information in your profile might come from properties your organization defines in its network's directory service (such as Active Directory). One example is the company hierarchy. In a My Site profile, the reporting structure you see for the organization can come from Active Directory.

Under your picture (or the generic image), click Edit My Profile to open a page on which you can provide information such as the following:

- Describe yourself in the About Me area.
- Upload a picture to share.
- Identify topics that your colleagues should ask you about.
- Add contact information. In this area, use the list in the Show To column to indicate who can view the information you provide in specific fields. You can choose Only Me, My Manager, My Team, My Colleagues, or Everyone.
- In the Details area, add information about projects you worked on, skills you have, schools you attended, and your birthday. You can also control who views the information you enter in this area.
- Use the Newsfeeds area to type a list of your interests. Also indicate whether to receive notifications in e-mail when someone leaves a note in your profile or adds you as a colleague and whether you want to receive suggestions for colleagues and keywords. In the list at the bottom of this section, clear the check boxes for any activities you don't want to follow.

To identify people you recognize as colleagues, click on the Colleagues tab on your profile page and then click Add Colleagues. Enter the name or e-mail address of a colleague in the Colleagues area (or browse in your address book). In the Add To Group area, choose whether to identify this person as part of your team. If you select Yes, this person can view information in your profile that is set up for team viewing. You can also add colleagues to groups. The General and Peers groups are provided by default. Use the New Group option to define a group of your own. At the bottom of the dialog box, use the Show To list to indicate who can see that this person is your colleague.

Use the Content tab to display the My Content page for your My Site. The My Content page provides document libraries to which you can upload documents for your own use or documents or pictures to share with other people.

On the Tags And Notes page, click a tag in the tag cloud to see which items the tag applies to. Use the Refine By Type menu to see only tagged content or only the content for which notes are entered. You can also filter for private or public tags.

Use the Tags And Notes page in the My Site user profile to see which content a tag is applied to.

➤ To update your My Site profile

1. Click your user name at the top-right corner of the team site.

2. Select **My Profile**.

3. Under your profile image, click **Edit My Profile**.

4. Add information that you want to include in your profile. Use the **Show To** lists to specify who can view the information. You can apply different settings to different fields.

5. Click **Save and Close**.

Sharing Your Site

If you have appropriate permissions, you can invite other users to share your team site. Use the Share Site command on the Site Actions menu to open the Share Your SharePoint Site dialog box. In the dialog box, enter the e-mail addresses for the people you want to invite. You can invite them to be part of the Team Site Visitors or Team Site Members group. If you want to send the invitation via e-mail, keep that option selected and type the message you want.

> **Tip** You can share your site with people outside your organization if your site is enabled for this feature. A site administrator must allow external users for the site collection and then activate the external users invitation feature.

➤ To share your site with other people

1. On the **Site Actions** menu, select **Share Site**.

2. In the **Share Your SharePoint Site** dialog box, enter e-mail addresses for the people you want to invite to share your site. You can add them as members or as visitors.

3. Type a message that will accompany an e-mail invitation.

4. Click **Share**.

Working with Groups and Permissions

SharePoint uses groups to manage access to the site and to control the scope of operations that members of a group can perform. In managing a site, you work with three main groups, which are Team Site Owners, Team Site Members, and Team Site

Visitors. By default, site owners have full control over a site. Members can contribute to the site (meaning they can upload and edit documents, among other tasks). Users in the Team Site Visitors group have read access to the site.

> **Tip** Placing users in groups and assigning permissions to the group rather than to individual users saves time managing the site because you can change group permissions when necessary instead of changing permissions for a number of individuals.

Managing Site Permissions

On the Site Settings page you open from the Site Actions menu, use the Site Permissions link under Users And Permissions to manage site permissions. The groups defined for the site are listed along with the permission level each group has. You can click a group name to see a list of the current members of that group.

The Grant Permissions button opens a dialog box in which you can add a user to a group or set the permissions level for a user or a group. In the Grant Permissions area of this dialog box, you can choose the group you want to add the user to (the recommended approach) or select an option to grant permissions directly. If you choose the direct path, you then specify the permission level:

- **Full Control**   The user has full control of the site. This is the default level granted to site owners.

- **Design**   The user can view, add, update, delete, approve, and customize items in the site.

- **Contribute**   The user can view, add, update, and delete list items and documents. This is the default level granted to the Team Site Members group.

- **Read**   The user can view pages and list items and download documents. This is the default level granted to the Team Site Visitors group.

- **View Only**   The user can view pages, list items, and documents. Document types that can be rendered in a browser can be viewed but not downloaded.

You can then type a message that accompanies a welcoming e-mail that SharePoint sends to the user.

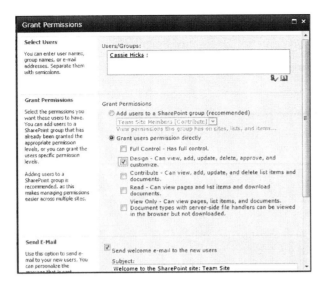

To administer permissions, it's best to assign users to groups. If you apply permissions directly, you need to select one of these options.

To change the permission level assigned to a specific group, select the group and then click Edit Permissions. In the dialog box provided, select the new permission level you want to assign to this group. If you no longer need a group, select the group and then click Remove Group Permissions.

> **Tip** To see the permission level granted to a specific user or group, click Check Permissions, type the name of the user or group, and then click Check Now. The Check Permissions dialog box then lists the group the user is a member of and the user's permission level.

Defining a Permission Level

The built-in permission levels and SharePoint groups will cover the needs of most team sites. You can define your own group (as discussed in "Creating a Group") and, if necessary, define your own permission level. On the Permission Tools Edit tab, click Permission Levels and then select Add A Permission Level. Type a name and description, and then work through the list of permissions you want this level to enjoy. The permissions are categorized under List Permissions, Site Permissions, and Personal Permissions. You can fine-tune the tasks that a site member granted this level can perform by taking this approach.

➤ **To grant permissions to a group or user**

1. On the **Site Settings** page, under **Users and Permissions**, click **Site Permissions**.

2. Click **Grant Permissions**.

3. Select the user or group.

4. Under **Grant Permissions**, select the group you want to add the user to, or select **Grant User Permission Directly**, and then select the permission level for the user.

5. If you send a welcome e-mail, type a message to accompany the e-mail and then click **OK**.

Creating a Group

If you want to create your own group with which to manage user permissions, click the Create Group button on the Permission Tools Edit tab. On the Create Group page, you work with the following fields and options:

- **Name And About Me Description**   Enter a name for the group, and describe the purpose of the group.

- **Owner**   By default, the person who creates the group is designated a group owner, but you can add other owners as need be.

- **Group Settings**   The options in this area control who can view group members and who can edit group membership. By default, only group members can see who is in the group. Choose Everyone for wider visibility. For editing group membership, the default setting is Group Owner, but you can choose to let group members manage membership as well.

- **Membership Requests**   In this area, choose options for managing requests to join or leave the group. By default, requests to join or leave are not allowed. To ease administration when conditions permit it, you can select Yes to allow requests and also select Yes to automatically accept requests. If you allow requests, provide the e-mail address where requests should be sent.

- **Give Permission To This Site**   The settings in this area grant the level of permission the new group will have. See the previous section, "Managing Site Permissions," for a description of these options.

When you click Create on the Create Group page, SharePoint displays a page you use to add members to the group. See the next section for information about adding users to a group.

➤ To create a group

1. On the **Permissions Tools Edit** tab, click **Create Group**.

2. Type a group name and description.

3. Add other group owners if necessary.

4. Under **Group Settings**, select settings for who can view group members and who can edit group membership.

5. Under **Membership Requests**, specify whether you want to allow requests for joining or leaving the group. If you select Yes to allow requests, specify whether you will accept auto requests and the e-mail address for the person who should receive requests.

6. In the **Give Group Permission To This Site** area, select the group's permission level.

7. Click **Create**, and then add members to the group.

Adding Users to the Site or a Group

You can add users to the Team Site Members group (the default group) by opening the Site Settings page, clicking People And Groups, and then clicking New, Add Users. This opens the Grant Permissions dialog box, in which you select the users you want to add to the site and type a message that accompanies an e-mail SharePoint can send to welcome the users.

To add a user to a different group, select the group in the Quick Launch and then choose the New, Add Users command. On the group page, you can use the Actions menu to remove a user from the group or call or send an e-mail to the group. If you choose to call the user, Microsoft Lync runs if it is not already started.

On the Settings menu, choose Group Settings to update group properties or, if necessary, to delete the group. You can also use this menu to view group permissions, make the group the default group, and open the List Settings page.

> **See Also** For information about list settings, see "Working with List Settings" later in this chapter.

➤ To add users

1. On the **Site Settings** page, click **People and Groups**.

2. In the Quick Launch, select the group you want to add users to.

3. Click **New, Add Users**.

4. In the **Grant Permissions** dialog box, select the users to add and type an e-mail message if you want to.

5. Click **OK**.

Creating a Site Template

You can develop the basic team site that comes with Office 365 by adding lists, libraries, pages, custom views, and other components. With these components in place, you can save your site as a template on which you can base other sites. For example, if you use your team site to manage a group of similar projects, add the elements you want to use for each project, save the site as a template, and then use that template whenever you start a new project.

> **See Also** As you'll learn later in this chapter in "Creating a Site," you can choose from a number of built-in site templates when you create a site.

Use the Site Actions menu to display the Site Settings page, and then click Save Site As Template in the Site Actions group. Enter a name for the template file (do not include an extension), a name and description for the template, and specify whether to include the content from the base site. You must select this option if you want to include custom workflows, but you should also include it if you have uploaded model documents to the site—for example, a budget or a presentation template.

You can apply this site template when you create a new site (click New Site on the Site Actions menu to start the process) by choosing it from the Blank & Custom category in the Create dialog box.

Templates you create are stored in the Solutions gallery. To manage custom templates, open the Site Settings page from the Site Actions menu and click Solutions in the Galleries area.

➤ **To create a site template**

1. Set up the site with the elements you want to include in the template.

2. On the **Site Actions** menu, click **Site Settings**.

3. In the **Site Actions** group, click **Save As Template**.

4. Type a file name, name, and description of the template.

5. Select **Include Content** if you want to include site content in the template.

6. Click **OK**.

Using List Templates

You can set up a list with custom views and standard items (for example, a set of tasks you perform for each program your team works on) and then save the list as a template. You can then base new lists on the template you create.

Use the Quick Launch or the All Site Content page to open the list you want to base the template on. Add items to the list you want to include in the template. For example, for a tasks list, add the standard tasks you want as part of your task list template. (See "Setting Up a Task List" later in the chapter for details.)

When the list is configured the way you want it, click on the List tab, and then click the List Settings button (at the right end of the ribbon) to open the List Settings page. Under Permissions And Management, click Save List As Template.

On the Save As Template page, type the file name for the list template (you should not include an extension) and the name and description for the template itself. If you want to include the content of a list in the template, select that option.

> **Tip** By default, you can create a list template that contains up to 10 megabytes (MB) of content. However, an administrator can increase this size limit.

If you need to edit the properties for a list template (to change its name, for example), open the Site Actions menu and choose Site Settings. Under Galleries, click List Templates. Select the list template and then click Edit Properties in the Manage group on the ribbon's Documents tab.

> **Tip** If you want to use a list template on a site that is in a different site collection, open the gallery of list templates from the Site Settings page (as just described). Select the template, and then click Download A Copy in the Copies group on the Documents tab. Now switch to the other site, open the list templates gallery, and then use the Upload Document command to add the copy of the template to that site.

➤ **To create a list template**

1. Display the list you want to use as a template.

2. On the **List Tools Library** tab, click **List Settings**.

3. In the **Permissions And Management** area of the **List Settings** page, click **Save List As Template**.

4. Type a file name, name, and description of the template.

5. Select **Include Content** if you want to include site content in the template.

6. Click **OK**.

Applying a Site Theme

If you have permissions to work with site settings and other configuration options, you can make changes to the appearance of your team site. For example, you can apply a theme to your site to display links (and followed links) in a different color. Themes also control heading and body fonts.

From the Site Actions menu, open the Site Settings page and then click Site Theme in the Look And Feel section. You can select one of the built-in themes or use the controls in the Customize Theme area to select the colors you want to apply to the array of elements listed (which include text/background colors, six accent colors, hyperlinks and followed hyperlinks, and the heading and body font). Use the Preview button to take a look at how the settings affect the site before you apply them.

Change the appearance of a site by applying a theme. You can customize the colors applied to different site elements.

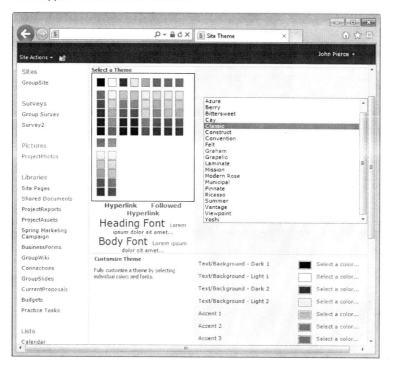

> **Tip** You can also use the shortcut under Getting Started on the site's home page to open the Site Theme page.

➤ **To apply a site theme**

1. On the **Site Actions** menu, click **Site Settings**.

2. Under **Look And Feel**, click **Site Theme**.

3. On the **Site Theme** page, select a built-in theme, or use the **Customize Theme** area to define theme elements of your own.

4. Click **Preview** to see your selections affect the appearance of your site.

5. Click **Apply** to display the new theme.

Changing the Appearance of a List

Lists come with three default forms: a form for new items, a form for editing items, and a form for viewing the items in the list. You can modify certain display properties of these forms and add web parts to the form to augment them.

Start by opening the list you want to work with. On the List Tools List tab, go to the Customize List group, click the arrow next to Modify Form Web Parts (use the ScreenTip to identify this button if you don't see the full label), and then select the form you want to work with.

When the form is displayed, use the Page Tools Insert tab to insert text, images, or other types of web parts. Switch to the Web Part Tools Options tab and click Web Part Properties to work with settings that control a web part's appearance, dimensions, and layout. Set the height and width of the web part in the Appearance section. Use the Chrome State and Chrome Type settings to specify whether the whole web part or just the title bar is displayed and whether the title bar and border of the web part are displayed.

Editing a Web Part Page

You can work with other web part pages in the same way that you work with the web parts that make up a list. Display the page you want to customize, and then select Edit Page on the Site Actions menu. You'll see the same set of tabs and commands as you do when you are modifying a list form or customizing a library. For more information, see "Customizing a Library" later in this chapter.

See Also You can also change the way a list is displayed by creating different views for the list. Creating and modifying views for lists are similar to how views are handled for libraries. For information about managing views, see "Managing Library Views" later in this chapter.

➤ **To update list forms**

1. Display the list you want to work with.

2. On the **List Tools List** tab, in the **Customize List** group, click **Modify Form Web Parts**, and then choose the list form you want to modify.

3. Click on the **Page Tools Insert** tab, and then use the options provided to add another web part to the page. (You can also click **Add A Web Part** where this link appears.)

4. To modify a web part, point to the top-right corner of the web part frame and select the check box. Click the arrow that appears, and then choose **Edit Web Part**.

5. Use the edit web part tool pane to make changes to web part properties.

6. In the tool pane, click **Apply** to see your changes. Click **OK** close the tool pane.

7. On the **Page** tab, click **Stop Editing**.

Creating a Site

Adding pages, lists, and libraries to your team site increases the scope of the work you manage through your site. You can also define additional sites (subsites) that are branches of your team site and use these sites for specific purposes. For example, you might tailor the base team site to create a company portal and then add subsites that divisions, departments, and teams use to manage their information and projects.

You can use a number of site templates as the basis of subsites. Choose New Site from the Site Actions menu to open the Create dialog box and then click on the Browse tab to see the list of templates.

> **Tip** You can use the Featured Item page in the Create dialog box to set up a new team site.

Use the links under Filter By to see all the types of site templates or the templates in a category. Enter a title for the site, and then click More Options to specify other site properties. These include a description of the site and the URL for the site, which stems from your Office 365 domain name.

By default, subsites inherit permissions from the parent site. Keep this option selected, or select Use Unique Permissions if you want to set up permissions for this site directly. Under Navigation, you can choose to display a link to this site on the Quick Launch and in the top link bar. In the Navigation Inheritance section, select Yes if you want to use the same top link bar as the parent site.

The following list summarizes templates by category. (Some templates are listed in more than one category in the Create dialog box but are not repeated here.)

- **Blank and Custom**
  - **Blank Site** Use this template to build a custom site. This template does not provide any lists or libraries by default.
  - **Personalization Site** Personalization sites are designed to help connect a portal to users' My Sites. The template can help identify the current user and present information that is specific to that user on the basis of the user's My Site profile.

- **Collaboration**
  - **Team Site** This template allows teams to author, organize, and share information. The Team Site template provides a document library and lists for managing announcements, calendar items, tasks, and discussions.
  - **Document Workspace** Use this template to create a site at which coworkers collaborate on a document. The template provides a document library for storing the primary document and supporting files, a task list, and a links list for related resources.

    > **See Also** You can also create a document workspace from a document library. See "Working with Document Copies" later in this chapter.

  - **Group Work Site** This template is designed for teams to create, organize, and share information. It includes a group calendar, a document library, and basic lists.
  - **Express Team Site** This template creates a slimmed-down team site that contains a document library and an announcements list.

- **Content**
  - **Blog** A blog is used to exchange ideas with people who visit the site.
  - **Document Center** A document center is a site where you can centrally manage documents.
  - **Visio Process Repository** This site is used to view, share, and store Visio process diagrams. It provides a versioned document library for storing diagrams and lists for managing announcements, tasks, and review discussions.

- **Meetings**
  - ○ **Basic Meeting Workspace**   This site template allows you to plan and organize a meeting, as well as record its results. It provides lists for managing the agenda, recording meeting attendees, and organizing meeting documents.
  - ○ **Blank Meeting Workspace**   This is similar to the Basic Meeting Workspace template. This template allows you to plan and organize a meeting and record its results, but it does not include default lists.
  - ○ **Decision Meeting Workspace**   This template allows you to track the status of a meeting or make decisions about it. It includes lists for creating tasks, storing documents, and recording decisions.
  - ○ **Social Meeting Workspace**   You can use this template for social occasions. It provides lists for tracking attendees, providing directions, and storing pictures of the event.
  - ○ **Multipage Meeting Workspace**   Like the Basic Meeting Workspace, this template is designed for planning and organizing meetings. It provides lists for managing the agenda and recording meeting attendees and two blank pages that you customize.

- **Search**
  - ○ **Enterprise Search Center**   The welcome page for this template provides a search box with two tabs: one for general searches, and another for searches for information about people. You can add and customize tabs for other search scopes or result types.
  - ○ **Basic Search Center**   The site includes pages for search results and advanced searches.
  - ○ **FAST Search Center**   The FAST Search Center template is set up the same as the Enterprise Search Center. Unlike the Enterprise Search Center, the FAST Search Center must be configured using the FAST Search engine, not standard SharePoint search.

- **Web Databases**

  The following templates use Microsoft Access to provide SharePoint sites with specific features:
  - ○ Assets Web Database
  - ○ Charitable Donations Web Database

   ○ Contacts Web Database

   ○ Issues Web Database

   ○ Projects Web Database

> **Important** Access Services must be enabled before you can use the Web Databases site templates.

➤ To create a site

1. On the **Site Actions** menu, click **New Site**.
2. In the **Create** dialog box, click **Browse All**.
3. Filter the templates displayed by selecting a category in the **Filter By** list.
4. Type a name and URL for the site, and then click **More Options**.
5. Add a description for the site.
6. Select **Use Unique Permissions** if you want to set up permissions for this site directly.
7. Select the navigation options you want to use, and specify whether the subsite should use the top link bar from the parent site.
8. Click **Create**.

Practice Tasks

Practice the skills you learned in this section by performing the following tasks on your site:

- Create a second team site as a subsite of your main site.
- Use the Site Settings page to view the permissions SharePoint sets up for the site.
- Use the Site Settings page to apply a theme to the site.
- Upload documents to the Shared Documents folder.
- Select one or more of the documents, and add tags and notes for it.
- Go to your user profile on My Site, and see how the notes and tags appear there.

4.3 Manage Site Content

Much of the content you store on a team site is organized in libraries and lists. Libraries are designed for specific purposes—from the general document library for storing all types of files to a slide library, which you can use to manage content you use regularly in Microsoft PowerPoint presentations. SharePoint also provides a number of list templates, including those for managing appointments and meetings, discussion boards, surveys, and tasks.

In this section, you'll learn about managing content in libraries and lists and about how you manage the libraries and lists themselves through a variety of settings. You'll also learn in detail about working in a document library and with a task list, a survey, and a discussion board.

Selecting the Library You Need

As you add components to your team site, you can create additional document libraries to store budgets, proposals, product descriptions, and the like. You can also create libraries that are set up to store specific types of content.

Libraries are defined in part by the columns used to identify and manage content. For example, a report library includes the columns Report Status and Report Category. In a picture library, you can see information such as the file size and the dimensions of the picture. Libraries are also associated with specific content types. A forms library is set up to create a Microsoft InfoPath form, for example. A report library provides commands to create a Microsoft Excel workbook or a web page on which you can display summarized information.

> **See Also** You'll learn more about working with content types in SharePoint libraries in "Working with Settings for Content Types" later in this chapter.

You can add the following types of libraries to your team site:

- **Document library**   Use a document library to store documents of various types. For the files you keep in a document library, you'll often keep track of versions to maintain a record of how a document changes over time. You might also enable a setting that requires users to check out a document to edit it exclusively and then check it in when modifications are in place.

> **See Also** You'll learn more about managing versions and checking documents out and in later in this chapter in "Using a Document Library."

- **Form library**   To store business forms that you create with a program such as Microsoft InfoPath, add a form library to your team site. The New Document menu item in a form library is set up to create an InfoPath form.

- **Picture library**   This library is designed for storing and sharing pictures. By default, picture libraries are placed in a separate section on the Quick Launch. You can view thumbnail images in the library. Double-click a thumbnail and then click Edit Item on the ribbon to add information about the picture.

- **Wiki page library**   This library provides pages that are designed for quick collaboration. The welcome page that SharePoint displays when you create a wiki describes how you might use the library—for brainstorming or gathering research notes, for example. Click on the Page tab, click Edit, and then use the commands on the Editing Tools tabs to add content and objects to the wiki pages.

> **See Also** You'll learn more details about wikis in "Using a Wiki Page Library" later in this chapter.

- **Asset library**   Use an asset library to store large media files, including images, video, and audio files. When you add an item to an asset library, you can choose the type of item from the New Document menu. SharePoint provides a dialog box in which you can provide a name and title, enter keywords for the item (which are used in searches), provide comments, identify the author, add a date and time stamp, and specify a copyright date.

- **Data-connection library**   A data-connection library is used to store files that let you connect to applications outside the team site and SharePoint. In this library, you can store an Office Data Connection (ODC) file or a Universal Data Connection (UDC) file. InfoPath can use a UDC file for connections. An ODC file can be used with a server application such as Microsoft SQL Server to help generate reports.

- **Report library**   A report library is designed for documents related to goals, business intelligence, and organizational metrics. In a report library, you can assign a report to a category, for example, and specify the status of a report.

- **Slide library**   Use a slide library to share slides that are included in Microsoft PowerPoint presentations. In a slide library, you can see a thumbnail of the slide as well as the presentation a slide is associated with. When you add a slide, you use the Publish Slides dialog box in PowerPoint.

> **Important** In the Office 365 Professional and Small Business plan, only document, picture, form, and wiki page libraries are available.

➤ **To create a library**

1. On the **Site Actions** menu, click **More Options**.

2. In the **Create** dialog box, apply the **Library** filter.

3. Select the type of library you want to create.

4. Type a name for the library.

5. Click **Create**.

Managing Library Views

Most types of libraries come with defined views. In a document library, the default view (and the only view available initially) is All Documents, and in an asset library, the default view is Thumbnails. In a report library, the default view is Current Reports, but two other options—All Reports And Dashboards and Dashboards—are available on the Current View menu, which you access in the Manage Views group on the Library tab. To change the view of a library, simply select the view you want from this menu.

Change the view for a list or a library by using the Current View menu. You can create public views or personal views and also modify the views SharePoint provides.

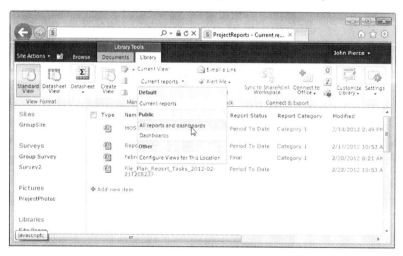

You can create other views for a library or modify the views that SharePoint provides. You might create a view to apply a specific filter or sort order to a library or to create a view that's designed for data entry (a datasheet view). When you create a view, you can choose a format as the basis of the view (you'll often use the format Standard View) or select one of the library's existing views as your starting point.

One of the first options you specify when you create a view is whether the view is a personal view or a public view. A public view is available to anyone viewing the library, and a personal view is available only to the user who creates it. All built-in views that SharePoint provides are public views.

> **Important** Some users might not have permission to create public views for a library, but these users can create personal views.

Use this page to create a view. Select the columns you want, and set the order in which the columns appear.

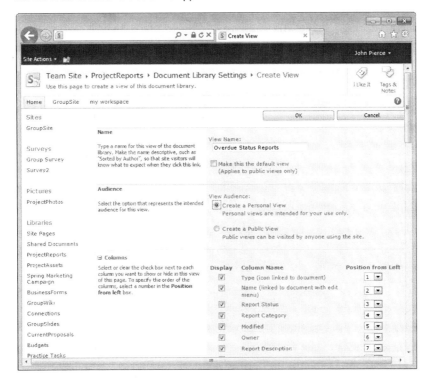

The Create View page provides a number of fields you use to define a view, and you might not need to change the default settings for many of these fields. The following list summarizes the fields you work with on the Create View page:

- **Name**   A view's name should briefly describe the view (All Reports, for example). You can select a check box to make this view the default view.

- **Audience**   Use this area to specify whether the view is a public or personal view.

- **Columns**   Use the check boxes to specify the columns to include in the view. Use the Position From Left list to set the column order.

- **Sort**   You can specify two columns to sort by. Choose the columns, and then select the option to sort in ascending or descending order. In a library, users can sort library items by using column headings. If you want to maintain the sort order specified for the view, select the option Sort Only By Specified Criteria.

- **Filter**   You can keep the default setting to show all items in a view or define a filter to view a selection of the items. To filter on a column based on the current date or the current user of the site, type **[Today]** or **[Me]** as the column value. You can also specify a date, for example, to see only files modified after that date. Filters are especially useful in large lists because they let users work with the list more efficiently.

- **Inline Editing**   Select Allow Inline Editing to place an edit button on each row. This button allows users to edit the current row in the current view without navigating to the form. Inline editing is available only on views that have their style set to Default.

- **Tabular View**   The Allow Individual Item Checkboxes option in this area is selected by default. These check boxes let users select multiple items to perform bulk operations, such as deleting more than one file.

- **Group By**   Specify one or two columns by which to group items. For example, you could group items under the Modified By field in a document library or the Report Status field in a report library.

- **Totals**   You can use this area to calculate summary information about items in a library. The functions available depend on the type of column. They include Count, Average, Maximum, and Minimum.

- **Style**   In a document library, the following styles are available: Basic Table; Document Details; Newsletter; Newsletter, No Lines; Shaded; Preview Pane; and Default. The Shaded style, for example, displays a colored background in alternating rows. The Preview Pane style groups items along the left side of the library, where you can highlight an item to view its details.

- **Folders**   Specify whether to navigate through folders to view items or to view all items at once. If the list or library is structured by items or files within folders, you can provide a view in which the items or files are displayed without the folders.

- **Item Limit**   Use an item limit to restrict the number of items shown in a view. You can set an absolute limit or allow users to view items in batches of the size you specify. By default, the number of items available for display in a document library is 30 per batch.

- **Mobile**   Adjust mobile settings for this view by enabling it for mobile access, making this view the default view for mobile access and adjusting the number of items to display in the List View Web part for this view. You can additionally set the field to be displayed in a mobile list simple view.

The Edit View page is similar to the Create View page. You essentially work with the same fields, which are populated with values that define the view in its current state. When you modify a view, you can change the view's name, change the order in which columns appear in the view, add or remove columns from the view, define a filter or a sort order, or specify settings for other view fields.

> **Tip** The Edit View page does not let you make a public view a personal view. Base a new view on one of the built-in views if you want to create a personal view that resembles a built-in view. You can delete a view by selecting the view, clicking Modify View, and then clicking Delete.

➤ **To create a view**

1. In the **Manage Views** group on the **Library** tab, click **Create View**.
2. Select the format you want to use, or select an existing view for the basis of the new view.
3. On the **Create View** page, type a name for the view, specify whether the view is personal or public, and then select the columns and the column order for the view.
4. Set other view settings as needed.
5. Click **OK**.

➤ **To edit a view**

1. In the **Current Views** list in the **Manage Views** group, select the view you want to modify.
2. Click **Modify View**.
3. On the **Edit View** page, update settings for the view.
4. Click **OK**.

Creating a Column

To provide another perspective on the items in a library, you can create your own column and add it to one or more views. In the Create Column dialog box, you first name the column and specify the column type. The options for the type of column include Single Line Of Text, Multiple Lines Of Text, Number, Currency, Date And Time, Lookup (which you can tie to another field on your site), and others.

To augment the views for lists and libraries, define a custom column. Column settings depend on the type of column you use.

Options in the Additional Column Settings area of the dialog box change depending on the type of column. These options give you a high degree of control over the properties of a column you create. For the Number type, for example, you use this area to do the following:

- Describe the column
- Specify whether the column is required (so that it must contain data)
- Enforce unique values for the column
- Set minimum and maximum values
- Set the number of decimal places
- Specify a default value
- Choose an option to show the value as a percentage
- Specify whether to add this column to all content types in the library
- Specify whether to add this column to the default view

You can also create a formula that is used to validate the data a user enters in the column. In a Date And Time column, for example, you could create a formula so that only dates later than today are valid in the column.

Custom columns are added to the library's default view if you keep that option selected in the Create Columns dialog box. They are not added automatically to other views defined for the library, but you can add them by modifying a view.

➤ **To create a column**

1. In the **Manage Views** group on the **Library** tab, click **Create Column**.

2. In the **Create Column** dialog box, type a name for the column and then select the column type.

3. In the **Additional Column Settings** area, type a description for the column and then specify other settings as required for the column.

4. Set up a validation formula if necessary.

5. Click **OK**.

Working with Library Settings

The Library Settings page is organized in several sections. (Click Library Settings on the Library tab to open this page.) The General Settings, Permissions And Management, and Communications areas appear at the top of the page. The links in these sections let you manage (among other settings) the library's name and description, default values for specific columns, versioning, permissions, and workflows associated with this library. Below these sections are the Columns and Views sections, and if the library is set up to allow multiple content types, you'll also see the Content Types section.

> **See Also** Many of settings you work with on the Library Settings page also relate to lists. For more information about these settings, see "Working with List Settings" later in this chapter.

In the following sections, you'll learn more details about library settings for workflows, versioning, and content types.

Workflow Settings

You can apply a workflow to the items in a library (or a list) to manage processes such as document approval. For example, you can apply a workflow to request for proposal (RFP) documents to ensure that the individual responsible for the proposal reviews it before the document is released. The three-state workflow, which comes with a team site, is one you can apply to approve a document as it is routed through various stages.

> **Important** To apply the three-state workflow to a library or the items in the library, you must add or define a Choice column for that library. You use the choices you define for that column as the states defined for the workflow. For more information, see "Creating a Column" earlier in this chapter.

Open the Workflow Settings page from the Permissions And Management area of the Library Settings page. Workflows associated with this library (which might be already defined by a site administrator) are listed at the top of the page. You can use the drop-down list to see which workflows apply to different item types in the library.

To define a workflow, first select the content type you want the workflow to apply to (or choose All to apply the workflow to the library itself). For example, for the standard Shared Documents folder, you can choose Document, Folder, or All. Next, click Add A Workflow.

On the Add A Workflow page, specify the workflow template (such as Three-State) and add the name you want to give to this workflow. You associate the three-state workflow with two lists: a task list (which can be the default list named Tasks or a different task list) and a workflow history list. You also need to select start options for the workflow. The default option is to allow an authorized user to start the workflow manually. You can elevate the permissions required by selecting the option Require Manage List Permissions To Start Workflow, and you can choose an option to start the workflow when an item is added to the library.

To complete the definition of the three-state workflow, click Next and then set up the workflow states by selecting a Choice column present in the library (Report Status, for example). You then specify values for each of the three states—Preliminary, Period To Date, and Final are the options presented for the default Report Status field in a report library.

To set up the three-state workflow, define the states and then set up e-mail notifications that site users receive when an item moves from state to state.

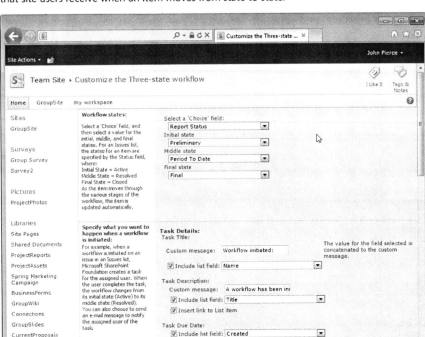

In the two Task Details sections, you define actions that occur when a workflow is initiated and when it reaches its middle state. You can set up an e-mail message to include information such as a task description and due date, who a task is assigned to, who the message goes to, and the subject line.

You can initiate a workflow (if the manual start option is selected) on an item by selecting it in the library and then clicking Workflows on the Documents tab. On the page SharePoint displays, under Start A New Workflow, click the workflow you want to apply to this item.

On the Workflow Settings page, you can see which workflows are in progress, add other workflows to the library, remove a workflow, and view workflow reports.

➤ **To view and manage workflow settings**

1. Open the library you want to work with.

2. Click on the **Library** tab, and then click **Library Settings**.

3. Under **Permissions And Management**, click **Workflow Settings**.

4. Use the drop-down list to see which workflows are configured to run on the different types of items in the library.

5. Use the links at the bottom of the page to add a workflow, remove a workflow, or view workflow reports.

Versioning Settings

Versioning lets you manage how content is added to and edited in a library. It also helps you keep track of the history of a document. You can, for example, keep a specific number of versions and you can choose to create both major and minor versions of a document. For tight control of a library, you can specify that an authorized user approve content that is submitted to the library and you can require users to check out a document before the document is edited.

In the General Settings area of the Library Settings page, click Versioning Settings to open a page that lets you control four aspects of versioning:

- In the Content Approval area, select Yes if you want items to be approved before they can be submitted to this library. If you select this option, you can then determine who can view draft items (items pending approval) in the library.

- Use the Document Version History settings to specify how to manage versioning. You can choose not to use versioning, to create major versions, or to create major and minor versions. You can also indicate how many major versions and drafts of major versions to retain.

- Under Draft Item Security, you indicate who can read draft items (which are defined as minor versions or items pending approval). The default option is Only Users Who Can Edit Items. You can broaden the scope of access by choosing Any User Who Can Read Items or tighten the process by choosing Only Users Who Can Approve Items (And The Author Of The Item).

- In the Require Check Out section, change the setting to Yes if you want to make it mandatory that users of the library check out a document before it can be edited. Requiring that users check out a document prevents editing conflicts because only one user (the user who checks out the file) can save changes to that file until the user checks in the file again.

> **See Also** For more information about versioning, see the following sections later in this
> chapter: "Managing Versions," "Publishing a Document," and "Checking Documents Out
> and In."

➤ To specify versioning settings

1. Open the library you want to work with.

2. Click on the **Library** tab, and then click **Library Settings**.

3. Under **General Settings**, click **Versioning Settings**.

4. Select the options you want to use for content approval, versioning, managing
   draft items, and requiring check out.

Working with Settings for Content Types

In libraries that are configured to allow multiple content types, you use the Library
Settings page to add and manage them. (To enable a library to use multiple content
types, on the Library Settings page click Advanced Settings in the General Settings area
and then select Yes for the option Allow Management Of Content Types.) Each content
type you define for a library can appear as an option on the New Document menu (you
have an option to hide these items), which lets users associate a document with the
content type when they create it.

To add a content type, click the link provided and then use the lists on the Add Content
Types page to select the content type you want to include in the library. You can choose
content types such as Audio, Basic Page, Picture, Report, and others.

Click Change New Button Order And Default Content Type to open a page that lets you
hide a content type from the New Document menu and change the order of the content
types—the first item listed is the default content type for the library.

➤ To manage content type settings

1. On the **Library** tab, click **Library Settings**.

2. On the **Library Settings** page, under **Content Types**, click **Add From Existing Site
   Content Types** to define a new content type for the library.

3. Click **Change New Button Order And Default Content Type** to set up the default
   content type or to specify that a content type does not appear on the **New
   Document** menu.

Using a Document Library

In this section, you'll learn how to create a document library and about the operations you perform when you work in the library.

Create a Document Library

Open the Site Actions menu and choose New Document Library to display the dialog box shown in the following screen shot. Use the dialog box to name and describe the library and select options for settings that affect navigation, versioning, and new documents you create from the library. By default, a link to a new document library is included on the Quick Launch. The default setting for versioning is No.

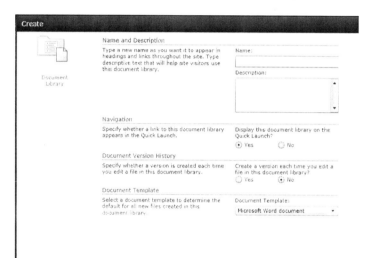

You can set options for navigation, versioning, and the default document type when you create a document library.

The document template you select specifies the type of document that's created by default when you use the New Document command in the library. You can choose options such as Microsoft Word Document (the default choice), Microsoft Excel Spreadsheet, and Basic Page (which creates a wiki page).

After you click Create in the dialog box, SharePoint displays the library with the Library tab selected on the ribbon.

> ➤ **To create a document library**
>
> 1. On the **Site Actions** menu, select **New Document Library**.
> 2. Type a name and description for the library.

3. Under **Navigation**, select **No** to not include a link to this library on the Quick Launch.

4. Under **Document Version History**, select **Yes** if you want to enable versioning in this library.

5. Under **Document Template**, choose the type of document that is created by default when you choose New Document in this library.

6. Click **Create**.

Create a Folder

Add a folder to a document library to help organize the files you store in it. Folders you add to a document library display the columns defined for the current view.

> **Tip** To navigate to the root of the document library, use the breadcrumbs. For more information, see Chapter 1.

➤ **To create a folder**

1. On the **Library Tools Documents** tab, click **New Folder**.

2. In the **New Folder** dialog box, type a name for the folder and then click **Save**.

Create a Document

When you create a document library, you specify a document template used to create new documents by default. In libraries in which more than one content type is defined, the New Document menu includes an entry for each type. Select New Document on the Documents tab, choose the type of document you want to create (if more than one option is provided), and then work with Word, Excel, or a page in SharePoint to define and create the document's content. When you save the document (in Word, for example), the path to the document library should appear in the Save As dialog box.

> **Tip** You might need to enter your Office 365 user name and password again before the application runs.

➤ **To create a document from a library**

1. On the **Documents** tab, click **New Document**.

2. If the library contains more than one content type, select the type of document you want to create.

Upload and Share a Document

Use the Upload Document command on the Documents tab to add one or more documents to the library. You can choose to upload a single document, or, depending on the browser you are working with, the Upload Document menu will also include an option to upload multiple documents. (The option to upload multiple documents is not supported in all browsers. It is available in recent versions of Internet Explorer.)

The Upload Document command opens a dialog box in which you browse to the location where the file is located. You can specify a destination folder within the library (if folders are defined) and add a note about the version of a file you are uploading (if versioning is enabled for the library).

When you choose to upload multiple documents, the dialog box you see lets you drag files or folders to it or browse for files by using the Open dialog box. The Upload Multiple Documents dialog box displays a progress indicator as the documents are added to the library.

➤ **To upload a single document**

1. On the **Documents** tab, click **Upload Document**.
2. In the **Upload Document** dialog box, browse to the file you want to upload.
3. Specify a destination folder if necessary, and add version comments if the library uses versioning.
4. Click **OK**.

➤ **To upload multiple documents**

1. On the **Documents** tab, click the arrow next to **Upload Document** and then choose **Upload Multiple Documents**.
2. In the **Upload Multiple Documents** dialog box, add files or folders by dragging, or use the link provided to display the **Open** dialog box and browse to the files.
3. Click **OK**.
4. When the documents are uploaded, click **Done** to close the dialog box.

Viewing and Editing Document Properties

You use the Manage group on the Documents tab to view and edit various document properties, including document permissions and version history.

Select a document in the library and click View Properties to open a dialog box that displays a document's name and title, for example. Click Edit Item in this dialog box to display a view of the dialog box in which you can update properties. You see the same view of the properties dialog box when you click Edit Properties on the Documents tab.

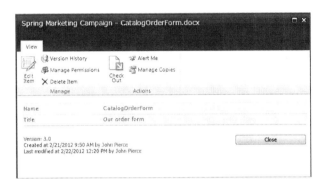

From this dialog box, you can manage document properties, versions of the document, and document permissions.

The View tab in the properties dialog box provides access to commands that let you manage properties. (These commands also appear in the Manage group on the Documents tab.)

- **Version History**   You can use the Version History dialog box to view, restore, or delete specific versions of a document. Be sure you look at the Comments field to see any notes entered about a specific version.

> **See Also** For more information, see "Managing Versions" later in this chapter.

- **Manage Permissions**   When you click Manage Permissions you open a page on which you can modify the permissions for this document. A notification bar indicates whether the document inherits permissions. Click Check Permissions to see the permissions that a specific user or group has for this document. Click Stop Inheriting Permissions if you want to create unique permissions for this document. (Adjustments you make to the permissions for the library will no longer affect this document.) After the page refreshes, you can modify document permissions as necessary. Use the Inherit Permissions button to reapply the library's permissions to this document.

> **See Also** For more information about managing and granting permissions, see "Working with Groups and Permissions" earlier in the chapter.

- **Delete the item**

> **See Also** You'll learn more about commands in the Action group in the properties dialog box later in this chapter.

➤ To edit a document's name or title

1. In the library, select the document you want to work with.

2. In the **Manage** group, click **Edit Properties**.

3. Make the updates in the fields provided, and then click **Save**.

➤ To view and manage document properties

1. In the library, select the document you want to work with.

2. In the **Manage** group, click **View Properties**.

3. To update the name or title of the document, click **Edit Item**, make the updates, and then click **Save**.

4. To view and work with a specific version of the document, click **Version History**.

5. To view or change permissions for the document, click **Manage Permissions**.

6. To remove the item from the library, click **Delete Item**.

Working with the Share & Track Group

The Share & Track group on a library's Documents tab contains just a couple of commands. You can use the E-Mail A Link command to open a new e-mail message (you might need to click Allow in a security dialog box before the message item opens) that contains a link to the document you select. (If you have more than one document selected, the E-Mail A Link command is not available.)

The Alert Me command lets you set up notifications you receive when a document is changed. You can be notified by e-mail or via text message (if your site is configured for text messaging). In the New Alert dialog box, you define a title for the alert (which you'll see in the subject line of an e-mail message you receive), specify the addresses to send the alert to, and the delivery method.

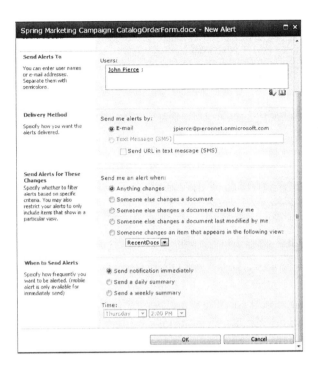

Specify the options for the event that triggers an alert and the timing for when you receive them.

You can choose one of five options for the event that triggers an alert:

- Anything Changes
- Someone Else Changes A Document
- Someone Else Changes A Document Created By Me
- Someone Else Changes a Document Last Modified By Me
- Someone Changes An Item That Appears In The Following View (Use the drop-down list to select the view you want to use.)

In the last section of the dialog box, choose an option for how often you want to receive alerts.

> **Tip** If you set up one or more alerts, choose Manage My Alerts from the Alert Me menu to open a page on which you can edit the settings for an alert, add other alerts, or delete an alert.

➤ **To send a link to a document via e-mail**

1. Select the document.
2. In the **Track & Share** group, click **E-mail A Link**.
3. Address the e-mail item, add any other information necessary, and click **Send**.

➤ **To set up an alert for a document**

1. Select the document, click **Alert Me**, and then choose **Set Alert On This Document**.

2. Enter a title for the alert (or use the default title).

3. Specify the people who should receive the alert.

4. Select a delivery method.

5. Choose an option for the event that triggers the alert.

6. Choose an option for when to receive the alert.

7. Click **OK**.

Checking Documents Out and In

As part of managing the content in a library, you can instruct or require users of the library to check out a file before the file can be edited. When a user checks out a file, that user has exclusive access to edit the file, but other users can still view the file. When a different user opens a checked-out file for editing, a notification appears informing the user of the file's status.

> **Tip** Checked-out files are indicated with a small, downward pointing arrow.

 You'll see this message when you open a file that is checked out to another user.

When a checked-out file is open in Word or Excel, for example, you can click on the File tab and then choose Check In to save changes to the library and make the file available for others. You can also save the file and then use the Check In command on the library's Documents tab. When you check in the document, type a comment about the changes you made. If you want to keep the file checked out, select Yes in the Retain Check Out area. You might use this option when you want other users to see the changes you've made up to this point but still retain editorial control over the document.

If you check out a file, make changes to the file, save those changes, but don't check in the file, you can restore the file to the state it was before you checked it out by choosing Discard Check Out.

> ➤ **To check out a document**

1. Select the document.

2. On the **Documents** tab, click **Check Out**.

3. Indicate whether you want to save a copy in your local drafts folder, and then click **OK**.

> ➤ **To check in a document**

1. On the **Documents** tab, click **Check In**.

2. In the **Check In** dialog box, select **Yes** in the **Retain Check Out** area if you want to keep the file checked out.

3. Enter a comment about the changes you made.

4. Click **OK**.

Managing Versions

If a library is set up to track document versions, you manage these versions in the Version History dialog box. In this dialog box, you can see each major version of a document that was published. You can use a menu to view the current version and to unpublish it. You can also view, restore, or delete a previous version. If you saved draft versions of the document, you can use a link in the dialog box to delete these versions. (They are moved to the site's recycle bin.) You can use the Delete All Versions link to send previous versions of the document to the site's recycle bin.

> ➤ **To manage versions**

1. Select the document.

2. In the **Manage** group on the **Documents** tab, click **Version History**.

3. In the **Version History** dialog box, point to a version and then use the drop-down menu to unpublish the most recent version, view the current version or a previous version, restore a version, or delete a version.

4. At the top of the dialog box, click **Delete All Versions** to send previous versions to the recycle bin.

5. Click **Delete Draft Versions** to send draft versions to the recycle bin.

Working with Document Copies

When you simply want to create a copy of a document on your computer—a copy that is no longer tied to the document library—click Download A Copy in the Copies group. (Note the text in the ScreenTip for the command that the copy you download will not be synchronized to the version in the document library.)

To create a copy of a document and place the copy in another SharePoint document library, click the arrow next to Send To and then choose Other Location. Paste in the URL for the library (or type the URL), type a new name for the copy (or use the current name), and specify an option for receiving a notification and an alert when the source document is checked in with changes.

When you create a copy of a document in another library, the copy is linked to the source document. The Copies group provides two commands you use to work with the copies you create in this manner. Click Go To Source to display a page that contains a link to the source document, a list of document properties, and commands you can use to manage the properties. On this page, you can open the document in your browser by clicking the document's name.

Click Manage Copies in the Copies group to see a list of copies linked to a document. Click Update Copies to synchronize the source file with the copy. Click New Copy to create a copy of this file in another document library.

Use this dialog box to update copies of a source document and to create new copies.

> ### ➤ To download a copy of a document

  1. Select the document.

  2. In the **Copies** group, click **Download A Copy**.

  3. Follow the instructions in your browser to save the copy.

> ### ➤ To send a copy to another location

  1. Select the document.

  2. In the **Copies** group, click **Send To** and then choose **Other Location**.

  3. In the **Copy** dialog box, complete the URL for the library you want to add the copy to.

  4. Modify the file name if you want to.

  5. Use the **Update** area to create an alert for changes made to the source document.

  6. Click **OK**.

7. In the **Copy Progress** dialog box, click **OK**.

8. When you see the indication that the file was copied successfully, click **Done**.

Creating a Document Workspace

The Send To command in the Copies group also includes the option Create Document Workspace. A document workspace is similar to a team site. It includes a Shared Documents library, a team discussion list, a calendar, an announcements list, and a task list. You can use the Create Document Workspace command to set up a document workspace (which becomes a subsite of the team site) when you want to work with a particular document and supporting files on a separate site.

The document is placed in the Shared Documents library in the document workspace. You can use the Documents tab to check out the document, edit its properties, download a copy, and so on. When you want to update the source library with the work you've done in the document workspace, point to the right of the document in the Share Documents list, use the arrow to open the menu, point to Send To, and then choose Publish To Source Location.

> **Tip** If you don't see the document workspace on the Quick Launch, click All Site Content at the bottom of the Quick Launch. In the Sites And Workspaces list, click the workspace you want to open.

➤ To create a document workspace

1. Select the document you want to use in the document workspace.

2. In the **Copies** group, click **Send To** and then choose **Create Document Workspace**.

3. On the **Create Document Workspace** page, click **OK**.

Sorting a Document Library

You can use the column headings to sort the items in a document library. In the Type column, you can sort in ascending or descending order or choose a file extension (SharePoint creates this list) to apply a filter that shows only the files associated with that extension. (Clear the filter when you want to see all items again.) You can sort by the Name column, and you can sort and filter items by using the Modified and Modified By columns. Point to the right of the column name, and then click the arrow to display the sorting and filtering options for that column. SharePoint displays an arrow (pointing up or down) to indicate the sorting column and sort order for the library. If you apply a filter, you'll see the filter icon beside the column name.

> **See Also** You can also specify settings for how a library is sorted by creating or modifying a view. For more information, see "Managing Library Views" earlier in this chapter.

➤ **To sort within a document library**

1. Point to the heading for the column you want to sort by.

2. Click the arrow to open the sort and filter menu.

3. Choose **Ascending** or **Descending** to specify the sort order.

4. If filters are available for the column, choose the filter you want to apply.

Publishing a Document

When versioning and content approval are enabled for a library, a minor version of a document (marked Draft in the Approval Status column) needs to be published to make the document generally available. The visibility of draft documents depends on the versioning settings.

> **See Also** See "Versioning Settings" earlier in this chapter for more information.

Clicking the Publish button on the Documents tab (in the Workflows group) opens the Publish Major Version dialog box. Use this dialog box to add a comment about the version you are publishing before you click OK.

> **Tip** If content approval is enabled for a library, publishing a draft document sets its status to Pending. A user with approval authority then needs to approve the document to change its status.

If you have permissions, you can unpublish a version to return a document to draft status.

➤ **To publish a document**

1. Select the document, and then click **Publish** in the **Workflows** group on the **Documents** tab.

2. In the **Publish Major Version** dialog box, type a comment to describe the version you are publishing and then click **OK**.

➤ **To unpublish a document**

1. Select the document, and then click **Unpublish** in the **Workflows** group.

2. Click **OK** to confirm the operation.

➤ **To approve or reject a pending document**

1. Select the document, and then click **Approve/Reject** in the **Workflows** group.

2. In the **Approve/Reject** dialog box, select the option you want under **Approval Status** (**Approved**, **Rejected**, or **Pending**) and then add a comment.

3. Click **OK**.

Coauthoring Documents

If you want to coauthor documents in SharePoint, do not set up the document library you'll work with to require that users check out a document before they edit it. That defeats the purpose of coauthoring.

You do not need to enable coauthoring, but (for the most part) you need to work with Microsoft Office 2010. You can coauthor documents in Word, Excel, PowerPoint, and OneNote.

You use the Excel Web App (rather than the Excel 2010 desktop client application) to coauthor worksheets. If you want to open an Excel file for coauthoring, select the file, open the shortcut menu at the right of the file's name, and then choose Edit In Browser. Changes you make to a worksheet in the Excel Web App are saved automatically. You'll see a notification at the bottom-right corner of the window telling you who is editing the file simultaneously.

The Excel Web App displays a message such as this when two or more people are working together on a spreadsheet.

In Word, you see online indications of where another author is working, and the status bar tells you how many authors have the document open. In PowerPoint, you also see notifications when someone else starts or stops editing a file you are working on. You can use the Info page on the File menu in Word or in PowerPoint to send an e-mail message or an instant message to someone working on a file with you.

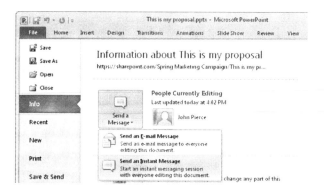

When you coauthor a document in Word or PowerPoint, you can communicate with other authors via e-mail or an instant message.

Customizing a Library

To change the layout of a library or to provide additional information by adding more web parts, you can customize it. First, open the page in edit mode by selecting Edit Page from the Site Actions menu. Choosing this command displays the Page Tools Insert tab and, when a web part is selected, the Web Part Tools Options tab.

Use the Insert tab to add a web part to the page. For example, choose a second document library to view on this page. To work with the properties of a specific web part, point to the top-right corner of the web part, select the check box, and then use the arrow that's displayed to open a menu and choose Edit Web Part. You'll then see the edit web part tool pane, which lets you specify views for the web part, change its appearance, and set other properties.

You can also click Add A Web Part in a free web part zone to open the gallery of web parts and choose one you want to add to the page.

When you finish customizing the page, click on the Page tab and then click Stop Editing.

➤ **To customize a library**

1. With the library open, click **Edit Page** on the **Site Actions** menu.

2. Click on the **Page Tools Insert** tab, and then use the options provided to add another web part to the page. (You can also click **Add A Web Part** where this link appears.)

3. To modify a web part, point to the top-right corner of the web part frame and select the check box. Click the arrow that appears, and then choose **Edit Web Part**.

4. Use the edit web part tool pane to make changes to web part properties.

5. In the tool pane, click **Apply** to see your changes. Click **OK** close the tool pane.

6. On the **Page** tab, click **Stop Editing**.

Connecting and Exporting in Libraries

The Connect & Export group on the Library tab provides a set of commands you can use to work with a library in other Office applications.

The Sync To SharePoint Workspace command lets you work with a library offline. (You'll learn more about this topic later in this chapter in the section "Working Offline with Content on Your Team Site.") You can use the Connect To Office command to add a shortcut to the document library to your Favorites list in Save As and Open dialog boxes in Word, Excel, and other Office applications. Use the Add To SharePoint Site command under Connect To Office to add the shortcut. You can also remove a shortcut or click Manage SharePoint Sites to display a page on which you can modify the shortcuts.

Click Export To Excel to create a list of the library's items (with column headings) in an Excel workbook. You might do this to create a tracking sheet or to cross-check an inventory of files.

Use the Connect To Outlook button to add this library to the navigation pane in Outlook. When you display the library in Outlook (by clicking the entry for it on the navigation pane, under SharePoint Lists), you'll see a list of the documents in the library. If the reading pane is open, a preview of the document is shown there. Double-click the document to edit it offline. If you are online when you save and close the document, you can update the copy in the SharePoint library.

➤ **To add a shortcut to a library to Office applications**

1. Open the library you want to work with.
2. On the **Library** tab, click **Connect To Office** and then click **Add To SharePoint Sites**.

➤ **To export a library to Excel**

1. Open the library you want to work with.
2. On the **Library** tab, click **Export To Excel**.
3. Follow the instructions in your browser to save or open the exported file.

➤ **To connect a library to Outlook**

1. Open the library you want to work with.
2. On the **Library** tab, click **Connect To Outlook**.
3. Click **Allow** in the security dialog boxes.
4. Click **Yes** in the message box Outlook displays.

Using a Wiki Page Library

To add a wiki page library to your team site, start with the More Options command on the Site Actions menu. After you add the library, the library's pages are listed in the Quick Launch. By default, a wiki page library sets up two pages: Home and How To Use This Library.

Before you can add content to a wiki page, you need to place the page in edit mode. Click the Edit button next the Browse tab at the top of the page. (You can also click on the Page tab on the ribbon and click Edit.) Work with the Editing Tools tabs to format text, apply styles, change layouts, and insert objects.

> **Tip** To work on a wiki page exclusively, check out the page before you edit it.

When you finish editing, click Save & Close in the Edit group (or use the icon at the top of the page).

To create a link to another page in a wiki library, enclose the name of the page in double brackets—for example, [[Recent News]]. After you type the first pair of brackets ([[), the library suggests page names on the basis of the characters you type. Finish the link by typing]]. Links do not become active until you save the page.

> **Tip** The page How To Use This Library contains examples of the types of links you can include.

You can use this linking mechanism to create a new page. Enclose the name of a page you want to create in the double brackets. When the link is active (links to pages that do not yet exist have a dashed underline), click it, and SharePoint displays the New Page dialog box. Just click OK to create the page.

> **Tip** You can also create a page by choosing New Page from the Site Actions menu.

Click View All Pages on the Page tab to view a list of the pages in the library. You can see a number of page properties, delete pages, view the version history of a page, and see who last modified the page.

Use the Page History button to open a page that shows a list of previous versions of a page. Recent changes are shown in the preview of the page. Click a link for a previous version to view it. Use the links at the top of that page to delete that version, restore the version, or view more information about the page's version history.

➤ **To edit a wiki page**

1. In the top link bar, to the left of the **Browse** tab, click **Edit**.

2. Use the **Page** tab to edit the page's properties, check out the page, rename the page, and perform other operations.

3. Use the **Editing Tools** tabs (**Format** and **Insert**) to add styles and formatting to the text, to change the page layout, and to insert objects such as images, tables, and web parts.

4. Use double brackets to create a link to pages in the wiki or to create a new page using the title you type between the brackets.

5. Click **Save & Close** when you finish working on the page.

Creating Pages

In addition to libraries (and lists, which you'll learn more about in the next section), you can add pages to your team site. You can add a basic page (such as you find in a wiki library) or a web part page, to which you add web parts to display information and provide additional features.

> **See Also** To learn about adding content to and editing a wiki page, see the previous section.

Basic pages you add to your team site are created in the Site Pages library, which you can open from the Quick Launch. You can add a basic page to your site by choosing New Page on the Site Actions menu.

To add a web part page, choose More Options from the Site Actions menu and then filter by Page in the Create dialog box. Select the Web Part Page option, and then click Create. To define the web part page, you need to enter a name, select a layout, and choose the library in which you want to store the web part page.

> **Tip** When you select a layout option, be sure to look at the thumbnail preview showing the page areas each layout provides.

When the new page is displayed, you'll see the page areas (also known as *web part zones*) outlined. To build the page, you need to add one or more web parts to the available zones. Use the Add A Web Part links to open a gallery of web parts to choose from. Use the Filter By list to see the web parts for each category listed. You can add a standard list or library type to a web part zone or a more specialized web part, such as an advanced search box or a view of information from Outlook Web App.

> **See Also** For information about editing web part properties, see "Customizing a Library" earlier in this chapter.

➤ **To add a basic page to the team site**

1. On the **Site Actions** menu, click **New Page**.

2. Type a name for the page, and then click **Create**.

3. Open the **Site Pages** library from the Quick Launch to start editing the page.

➤ **To add a web part page to the team site**

1. On the **Site Actions** menu, click **More Options**.

2. In the **Create** dialog box, click **Page** in the **Filter By** list.

3. Select **Web Part Page**, and then click **Create**.

4. On the **New Web Part Page** page, type a name, select the layout you want to use, and select the library in which you want to store the page.

5. Click **Create**.

6. In the page's web part zones, click **Add A Web Part**, and then choose the web part you want to include from the gallery that SharePoint provides.

Working with Lists

SharePoint lists are designed for specific purposes—posting announcements, tracking appointments and events, holding discussions, assigning and monitoring group tasks, conducting surveys, and many others. The following types of lists are available:

- **Announcements**   Use an announcements list for short status reports, event news, reminders, and similar information.

- **Calendar**   Maintain a record of team appointments, meetings, schedules, and events in a calendar list. Information in a SharePoint calendar can be synchronized with Microsoft Outlook.

- **Contacts**   Track information about customers, suppliers, vendors, and other people your team works with. Information in a SharePoint contact list can be synchronized with Microsoft Outlook.

- **Custom List**   Start with a blank custom list, and then add columns and views of your own.

- **Custom List In Datasheet View**   A blank list that's displayed as a datasheet (like a table in Microsoft Access or an Excel worksheet) to which you add your own columns and views.

- **Discussion Board**   Add a discussion board to your team site to collect opinions and thoughts about specific topics or processes. Discussions are organized in threads, and you can configure this list so that postings must be approved.

- **External List**   This list lets you view the data in an external content type.

- **Import Spreadsheet**   Use this list to include information from an Excel worksheet or another type of spreadsheet.

- **Issue Tracking**   An issue-tracking list is handy for managing projects. You can collect information about items that need resolution or require new resources. Items in an issue-tracking list can be assigned to individuals and given a priority and a status.

- **Links**   A list of web pages or other resources.

- **Project Tasks**   A project tasks list provides a view of items in a Gantt chart (like Microsoft Project).

- **Status List**   List personal or team goals in this list and then track their status. Color indicators mark progress.

- **Survey**   Use a survey to collect data and responses about issues and processes.

- **Tasks**   Keep track of the things that need to get done.

> **Tip** If you create any custom list templates of your own, those templates are included here as well. For details, see "Using List Templates" earlier in the chapter.

> **See Also** Later in this chapter, you'll learn more about working with a task list, a survey list, and a discussion board.

➤ **To create a list**

1. On the **Site Actions** menu, choose **More Options**.

2. In the **Create** dialog box, select **List** in the **Filter By** list.

3. Type a name for the list.

4. To enter a description of the list, choose a navigation option, and specify other properties of the list, click **More Options**.

5. Click **Create**.

   You won't need to enter a name before you click Create if you select External List or Import Spreadsheet.

Working with List Settings

To make changes to a list's properties and configuration, you work on the List Settings page. You might, for example, need to change the name of the list, set or update versioning settings, save the list as a template, or modify permissions for the list.

In the General Settings area, you work with the following settings:

- **Title, description, and navigation**   Update the list name and description, and specify whether to include a link to the list on the Quick Launch.

- **Versioning settings**   Control settings for content approval, item version history, and who can view draft items. For more information, see "Versioning Settings" earlier in this chapter.

- **Advanced settings**   Select options for managing content types, attachments, search visibility, bulk editing, and other operations.

- **Validation settings**   Create a formula to validate data for one or more columns in the list. For example, you could create a formula for the Due Date column that requires its value to be later than or equal to the value in the Start Date column. You can also define a message that explains validation criteria to users.

- **Rating settings**   If you want the users of a list to be able to rate the items it contains, open this page and enable rating settings. The list is updated with additional fields that allow users to rate the item. You'll also see the average rating and the number of ratings.

- **Audience targeting settings**   Use this link to enable audience targeting for the list. The audience targeting feature, which is configured through the SharePoint Online Administration Center, lets an organization target content to specific audiences.

- **Metadata navigation settings**   These settings help users find items in lists with many items by combining a tree control for navigation with filters based on specific fields.

- **Per-location view settings**   You can use this page to configure which views are available in a folder in the list, for example.

- **Form settings**   Use this option to use Microsoft InfoPath to change the design of a form associated with the list.

In the Permissions And Management area, use the following options to configure list settings:

- **Delete this list**   Click this link to delete the list.

- **Save list as template**   Create a template from the list. For more information, see "Using List Templates" earlier in this chapter.

- **Permissions for this list**   Use this link to change the permissions for the list.

- **Workflow settings**   On the Workflow Settings page, you can add a workflow to a list, view workflow reports, and associate a workflow with a specific type of item in the list (a task or a summary task, for example).

- **Generate file plan report**   A file plan report summarizes information about the list's configuration, providing information about available content types, permissions, number of items, and more.

- **Enterprise Metadata and Keyword Settings**   This link lets you add an enterprise keywords column to a list, which lets users enter keywords that are shared with other users and applications to facilitate searches and filters.

- **Information management policy settings**   From this link, you can select a type of list item and then define policies that set conditions for how items of that type are retained.

Under Communications, click RSS Settings to enable information from this list to be sent via an RSS feed.

In addition to these settings, you can use the List Settings page to configure content types for the list, to create a column or change the properties of columns, and to define and modify views.

> **See Also** For more information about columns and views, see "Creating a Column" and "Managing Library Views" earlier in this chapter.

Adding and Managing List Items

Use the New Item command on the List Tools Items tab or the Add New Item link at the bottom of the list when you want to add an item to the list.

In the New Item dialog box, fill in the fields that make up the list. The specific fields will vary depending on the type of list. For example, after you type a name for the item, you might need to specify relevant dates, set an initial status for the item, or start a new discussion topic by specifying the subject and substance of the initial posting.

The fields on a New Item form depend on the type of list. For an issues list, you can make assignments, set a status and priority, and specify related issues.

When you need to make changes to an item, select it in the list and then click Edit Item. To remove an item from a list, select the item and click Delete on the Items tab.

➤ **To add an item to a list**

1. On the **Items** tab, click **New Item**.
2. In the **New Item** dialog box, type a title for the item.
3. Fill in and specify other item settings. These vary depending on the type of list.
4. Click **Save**.

➤ **To edit an item in a list**

1. Select the item in the list, and then click **Edit Item** in the **Manage** group.
2. Update settings for the item, and then click **Save**.

➤ **To delete an item from a list**

1. Select the item in the list.
2. In the **Manage** group, click **Delete Item**.

Setting Up a Task List

A task list is defined by the following columns:

- Type (which can be either a task or a summary task)
- Title
- Assigned To
- Status
- Priority
- Due Date
- % Complete
- Predecessors

You can work with the default task list (named Tasks) that a team site provides when you create the site or create other task lists for specific purposes—perhaps one task list per project.

When you add an item to the list, use the New Item menu on the Items tab to select Task or Summary Task. (Choosing Summary Task essentially creates a folder in which you can nest specific task items.)

Fill in the fields with the information you have to date. The only required field for a new task item is the task's title, but you might also know about a task's assignment, priority, due date, and predecessors when you create it. The default status for a task is Not Started.

Use the Edit Item command to update information about a task as work on it progresses. You might change its status or priority or specify the percentage complete.

On the List Tools List tab, use commands in the Connect & Export group to work with the list in other Office applications. Use the Export To Excel command to create a worksheet from the task list. This step might be helpful for analysis and for creating summaries. Use the Connect To Outlook command to create a copy of this task list in Outlook.

Organizing a Survey

When you add a list based on the Survey list template to your team site, click the More Options button in the Create dialog box to describe the survey and to choose survey options. The first of these options controls whether user names appear in survey results.

The default setting is Yes. Select No if you want to grant people more confidentiality. The second option specifies whether people can reply to the survey more than once. By default, multiple responses are not allowed.

You can use a variety of field types when you define survey questions. The default type is Choice, which lets you define a set of possible answers from which respondents select. You might use other types of questions, such as Rating Scale, Yes/No, or Single Line Of Text, in surveys as well. If you want users to be able to add comments, choose Multiple Lines Of Text as the question type. The choice you make in the Question And Type area determines what other information you provide in the section Additional Question Settings.

Using Choice as the question type, you build a survey by typing the wording of the question and then using options in the Additional Question Settings area to list the choices for answers and configure how the choices will be presented—in a drop-down menu, as radio buttons, or as check boxes.

Under Additional Question Settings, you also do the following:

- Specify whether a question is required. (No is selected by default.)
- Specify whether to enforce unique values. (No is selected by default.)
- Specify whether users can fill in their own values. (No is selected by default.)
- Enter a default value if one is needed.

You can also include branching logic for a survey. For example, if a user selects choice B in one question, the survey displays a question related to that choice. You can also set up a formula that validates the data that is entered.

Click Next Question to set up additional questions for the survey, and click Finish after you define the survey's last question.

When you click Finish, SharePoint shows the settings page for the survey. You can adjust settings for the list and also use the links in the Questions area to add more questions or change the order of the questions.

People who take the survey open the list and click Respond To This Survey. The survey page shows when the survey was created and how many responses have been submitted. Use the links at the bottom of the page to review information about responses.

Running a Discussion Board

A team site provides a discussion board (Team Discussion) by default. You can use the Team Discussion list to learn more about discussion boards generally, and then add other discussion boards to the site as you need to.

Discussion boards include four columns by default: Subject, Created By, Replies, and Last Updated. When you add a discussion item to the list, you fill in the subject and the body of the item. You can attach files to a discussion item, and in the Body section of the New Item dialog box, you can use the ribbon to format the text, add hyperlinks or pictures, insert a table, and so on.

To read a discussion thread, click the entry in the list. You can sort the thread by who posted items. Click Reply to add your thoughts to the discussion thread.

Because a discussion board is a type of list, you can set up an alert for the list, create and modify views, and update other list settings.

Working Offline with Content on Your Team Site

SharePoint Workspace 2010 is an application that lets you work offline with content that's stored on your team site. SharePoint Workspace comes with the Professional edition of Office 2010.

You can synchronize the full team site or specific lists or libraries. To work with a list offline, open the list and then click Sync To SharePoint Workspace in the Connect & Export group on the List tab. (If you have not set up an account in SharePoint Workspace, the application will display a dialog box in which you can enter your name and e-mail address.)

In the Sync To SharePoint Workspace dialog box, click OK to proceed or click Configure to open a page on which you can select a different list or library (if that's necessary) or choose to download no content rather than all items in the list. You'll see a dialog box as the content is downloaded and synchronized to your computer. When this process is complete, click Open Workspace.

By synchronizing your site, a list, or a library with SharePoint Workspace, you can work with the content of your team site when you are offline.

In SharePoint Workspace, you can view the items in the list you chose to synchronize. Double-click an item in the main area of the SharePoint Workspace window to edit and update the information it contains. On the SharePoint Workspace Home tab, use the New command in the Items group to add items to the list. SharePoint Workspace will synchronize the lists when you connect to your team site again.

> **Tip** To synchronize the full team site with SharePoint Workspace, choose Sync To SharePoint Workspace on the Site Actions menu.

You can also connect to a site, list, or library on your site when you are working in SharePoint Workspace. On the File tab in SharePoint Workspace, click New, SharePoint Workspace. To connect to a site, select the site and then click OK. To set up a workspace for a specific list or library, click the Configure button, and then choose the library or list you want to connect to.

You can open a file from SharePoint Workspace when you are offline and make changes to that file. If someone else who is connected to your team site edits the same file before you connect again, that creates a conflict. If a conflict occurs, when you connect to your network again and SharePoint Workspace synchronizes with the site, SharePoint Workspace displays a tab named Error Tools Resolve. Click on that tab, and then click Resolve Conflict Or Error. In the dialog box that is displayed, you can choose which version of the file to accept or choose to keep both versions.

➤ **To synchronize a list with SharePoint Workspace and work offline**

1. On the **List** tab, in the **Connect & Export** group, click **Sync to SharePoint Workspace**.

2. In the **Sync to SharePoint Workspace** dialog box, click **OK**.

   After you synchronize your first list or library with SharePoint Workspace, you won't see this dialog box. Instead, SharePoint Workspace opens.

3. When you are offline, update items in SharePoint Workspace by double-clicking items in the list and using the **New** command on the **Home** tab.

4. Connect to your team site again when you can so that SharePoint Workspace can synchronize the content.

Practice Tasks

Practice the skills you learned in this section by performing the following tasks on your site:

- Create a document library named Practice Tasks, which you can use to test the skills you learned in this section. Set up the library for versioning. Also, add a wiki page library to your site, a survey list, and separate task list.

- Create a personal view based on the All Documents view. Include the columns Checked Out To and Check In Comment.

- Use the Library Settings page to configure versioning for major and minor versions. Let users who can edit items in this library see draft items.

- Upload six to ten documents to the library. Use the column headings to sort and filter the library.

- Create alerts for several of the documents.

- Open the wiki page library, and create one or more pages by using brackets.

- Add web parts to one of the wiki pages, and experiment with settings you change in the edit web part tool pane.

- Add three or four standard task items to the new task list, and then save that list as a list template.

- Create a survey. If possible, have other people in your organization respond to the survey. You can then view the summary results.

Objective Review

Before finishing this chapter, be sure you have mastered the following skills:

4.1 Search for site content

4.2 Manage sites

4.3 Manage content

Index

Symbols
[[ ]] (double brackets), 180

A
accessibility settings, 86
Access Services, 153
Account page, 78–80
  Connected Accounts, 79–80
  My Account, 79
Actions menu (Outlook Web App), 40–41
activity feeds, 123
Activity Feeds list, 94, 123
  presence information, 122
Add A Permission Level command, 143
Add A Web Part command, 178, 182
Add A Web Part links, 181
Add A Workflow page, 162
Add Colleagues command, 140
Add Filter To Favorites button, 42
Add New Account Wizard, 11
Add New Item link, 185
Add New Task button, 73
address books, 34
  external contacts, adding, 66
  global, 65
  opening, 35
  public groups in, 69
Add This Calendar link, 57
Add To SharePoint Site command, 179
administrators
  Admin page, 5
  contact preference settings, 16
  custom e-mail retention policies, 82
  external contacts, adding to shared address book, 66
  external users, allowing, 141
  Help For Admins, 19
  profile information, entering, 16
  public groups, setting up, 69
  public website, editing, 16
  SharePoint site permissions, 131
Admin link, 5
Admin page, 5
advanced searches, 133–135
  options for, 134–135

Alert Me command, 170–171
alerts
  configuration options, 96
  triggers, 171
Allow Management Of Content Types command, 165
All Site Content link, 31
All Sites searches, 133
Always On Top option, 128
announcements lists, 182
Appear Away status, 122
applications
  accessing, 3
  navigating, 26–32
appointments
  all-day events, 51
  controls for, 51
  fields in, 51
  recording, 50–52
  reminders, 51, 62
  Show Time As list, 51
Approve/Reject dialog box, 177
Ask A Question In The Forums link, 22
asset libraries, 155
Assets Web Database template, 152
Attach File command, 44
attachments, 35
  adding to conversation window, 105
  adding to e-mail messages, 44–45
  adding to task items, 74
  contact information in, 67
  deleting, 44
  exchanging in Lync, 98
  in instant messages, 114
  opening, 45
  saving, 45
  viewing, 44–45
  working with, 44–45
audience targeting, 184
audio conferencing, 115
audio devices, configuration options, 97
authentication, 4
Automatically Filter Junk E-Mail option, 89
automatic e-mail replies, 80–81
Automatic Replies page, 80

available information, 6. *See also* presence information
Available status, 122

B

background color of instant messages, 92
Basic Meeting Workspace template, 152
basic pages, adding to team site, 181–182
Basic Search Center template, 152
Be Right Back status, 122
Blank Meeting Workspace template, 152
Blank Site template, 151
Blocked Contacts, 120
blocked senders, 88–90
Blocked Senders list, 89
Blog template, 151
boldface elements in book, xi
book conventions, xi
breadcrumbs
    navigating with, 32
    root of document library, navigating to, 167
busy information, 6, 51
Busy status, 122

C

calendar lists, 182
Calendar Permissions dialog box, 57
calendars
    access level settings, 59
    adding, 60
    appearance options, 85
    appointments, 50–52
    categories, 60–61
    configuration settings, 85–86
    creating, 56
    default, 56
    flagging items, 61–62
    group calendars, 57
    meeting requests, 52–54
    notification settings, 85
    Other Calendars group, 60
    People's Calendars group, 57, 60
    publishing, 58–60
    reminders, 62–64, 86
    Scheduling Assistant, 55–56
    sharing, 56–58
    sharing permissions, 57–58
    time span settings, 59
    viewing, 57
    views, 50, 64
Calendar view, 50–64
    navigating in, 28–29
Call button, 117

call logs in Conversation History folder, 94
calls
    continuing, 124
    missed calls, viewing, 124
    recording, 98
    responding with instant message, 113–114
    video, 116
    VoIP, 115
categories (Outlook), 60–61
    assigning items to, 61, 63
    built-in, 60
    for contacts, 66
    creating, 63
    searching by, 72
Category command, 41
change alerts on documents, 170–171
Change Category Color command, 61
Change Conversation Subject command, 129
Change Font dialog box, 92
Change New Button Order And Default Content Type command, 165
Change Password page, 17
Change Privacy Relationship command, 120–121
Change Sharing Permissions command, 57–58
Charitable Donations Web template, 152
Chat command, 66, 114
checking files out and in, 172–173
Check Out Our Blog link, 23
Check Permissions dialog box, 143
Clear Filter button, 42, 43
Clear Flag command, 62
coauthoring documents, 177
collaboration, 13. *See also* SharePoint Online
    desktop, sharing, 101–102
    group conversations, 100–108
    meetings, online, 109–112
    opinion polls, 107–108
    PowerPoint presentations, sharing, 102–105
    programs, sharing, 106–107
    tags and notes for, 136–138
    whiteboards, sharing, 108
Collaboration templates, 151
Colleagues contacts, 120
columns, list
    creating, 159–161
    in discussion boards, 189
    enterprise keywords column, 185
    in libraries, 154
    in task lists, 187
    validation settings, 184
    in views, 157
community forums, 22–23
Community links, 7–8
Community page Forums link, 22

conference calls
  configuration settings, 96
  starting, 115
  with contact groups, 117
connected e-mail accounts, 79–80
  deleting a connection, 79
Connect & Export group, 179
Connect To Office command, 179
Connect To Outlook command, 179, 187
contact groups, 117–119
  adding contacts, 118–119
  communicating with members, 117
  creating, 117
  editing and managing, 119
  finding contacts, 118
contact list (in Excel), 71
contact list (Lync), 117–125
contact lists (SharePoint), 182
contacts
  adding, 65–66
  adding to distribution lists, 69–70
  adding to groups, 117
  Blocked Senders list, 89
  categories of, 120
  communicating with, 118
  conversation history with, 123–125
  deleting, 67
  duplicates, 71
  editing information, 67
  e-mailing, 66
  external, 65
  filtering, 30
  flagging, 61–62
  forwarding information on, 67
  groups, creating, 68–69
  importing, 71
  information about, 65, 66
  instant messages, sending to, 112–115
  inviting to group conversations, 100–101
  managing, 29–30, 65–72
  phone information, 95–96
  photographs of, 94–95
  privacy relationships, 93, 118–121
  Safe Senders And Recipients list, 89
  searching, 72, 118–119
  status settings, 122
  storage settings, 94
  trust levels for, 89
Contacts folder, 29
Contacts view, 65–72
  navigating in, 29–30
Contacts Web Database template, 153
content. See also libraries; lists
  adding to wiki pages, 180
  managing, 154–191

notes and tags, adding, 136–138
offline access to, 179, 189–190
searching, 132–136
versioning settings, 164–165
content approval, 164, 176
Content templates, 151
content types, defining, 165
context-sensitive Help content, 20–21
context-sensitive search scope, 132–133
Contribute permission, 142
conventions of book, xi
Conversation History folder, 94, 124
  viewing, 125
Conversations button, 124
conversations (Lync), 100–108
  changing subject, 129
  deleting, 125
  history, turning off, 99
  history, viewing, 123–126
  taking notes on, 128–129
conversations (Outlook Web App)
  configuration options, 85
  ordering of, 40
  reviewing, 38–39, 41
conversation window
  attachments, adding, 105
  dragging files to, 106
Create Column dialog box, 159–161
Create Document Workspace command, 175
Create Group button, 144
Create New Category command, 61
Create View page, 157–158
Ctrl+Alt+Spacebar keyboard combination, 101
Ctrl+N keyboard combination, 34
Customer Experience Improvement Program, 92
custom lists, 182
  in datasheet view, 182

D

data-connection libraries, 155
datasheet lists, 182
Decision Meeting Workspace template, 152
Default Reply Address list, 79
Delete All Versions command, 173
Delete Category command, 61
Delete Draft Versions command, 173
delivery reports, 81
Delivery Reports page, 81
Design permission, 142
desktop applications, configuring for Office 365, 9–11
desktop, sharing, 101–102
Discard Check Out command, 172
discussion boards, 183, 188–189

distribution lists
members, 70
membership approval options, 70, 83
ownership information, 70
setting up, 69–71
Document Center template, 151
document libraries, 14, 154, 166–179. *See*
also **libraries**
connecting, 178
creating, 166–167
customizing, 178
document properties, managing, 168–170
documents, checking out and in, 164, 172–173
documents, creating, 167
documents, uploading, 168
exporting, 178
folders, adding, 167
My Content page, 140
offline access, 179
Share & Track group, 170–172
sorting, 175–176
styles, 158
documents
approving content, 177
change alerts, 170–172
checking out and in, 164, 172–173
coauthoring, 177
copies, downloading, 173–174
creating in library, 167
draft items security, 164
e-mailing link of, 170–171
permissions, managing, 169
properties, managing, 168–170
publishing, 176–177
sending to another location, 174–175
source document link, 174
unpublishing, 177
uploading, 168
uploading to library, 32
versioning settings, 164–165, 169, 173
document workspaces, 151, 175
Document Workspace template, 151
Do Not Disturb status, 122
double brackets ([[ ]]), 180
Download A Copy command, 173
Downloads page, 7
information on, 9
draft items security, 164

E

Edit Properties command, 169
Edit Rule dialog box, 48
Edit View page, 159

e-mail
addresses, verifying, 35
attachments, 35, 44–45
automatic replies, 80–81
Blocked Senders list, 89
blocking and allowing messages, 88–90
checking names, 86
commands for, 41
configuration options, 84–85
connected accounts, 79–80
contact information, attaching, 67
conversations, 38–39, 41, 85
creating and sending messages, 34–37
Default Reply Address list, 79
delivery reports, 81
filtering messages, 41–42
flagging messages, 61–62
formatting messages, 36
forwarding messages, 40–41
forwarding Office 365 messages, 79
image attachments, 35
importance levels, 35
inbox rules, 45–50
managing, 33–50
marking messages as read, 84
message format, 36, 84
message options, 36, 84
mobile phone, sending and receiving on, 86–87
Office 365 account, 79
organizing, options for, 80–82
reading pane settings, 84–85
read receipts, 84
replying, 40–41
responding with instant message, 113–114, 115
retention policies, 82
reviewing, 37–41
Safe Senders And Recipients list, 89
saving drafts, 35
searching messages, 42–44
signatures, 35, 84
sorting messages, 39–40
spelling checker, 36, 85
To and Cc lines, 34
E-Mail A Link command, 170
e-mail message window
formatting toolbar, 34, 36
notification bar, 36
toolbar, 34–36
emoticons, 92
enterprise keywords columns, 185
Enterprise Search Center template, 152
enterprise version of Office 365, 9
three-state workflows, 14

Excel
    checking in documents, 172
    contacts list, 71
    libraries, exporting to, 179
Excel Web App, coauthoring documents in, 177
Exchange ActiveSync, 86–87
Export To Excel command, 179, 187
Express Team Site template, 151
external contacts, 65
    adding to address book, 66
    free and busy information, 55
External Contacts, 120
external lists, 183
external users, sharing team site with, 141

F

FAST Search Center template, 152
Favorites list
    document library shortcut, 179
    filtered views, adding, 42
    managing, 27–28
file plan reports, 185
file saving paths, 98–99
filtering
    activity feeds, 123
    contacts, 30
    e-mail messages, 41–42
    libraries, 158, 175–176
    task list, 30
Filter menu (Outlook Web App), 41
Find Previous Conversations command, 124, 125
Flagged Items And Tasks folder, 30
flags
    duration, 61
    removing, 62
    setting, 61–63
folders
    in document libraries, 167
    mailbox, 42
form libraries, 155
forms, 184
Forward As Attachment command, 40, 67
Forward button, 40
forwarding Office 365 messages, 79
free and busy information
    display of, 94
    for meetings, 55
    publishing, 59
    sharing, 56
Frequent Contacts group, 117, 118
Friends And Family contacts, 120
From command, 41
Full Control permission, 142

G

Getting Started topics, 21–22
Give Control command, 101, 106–107
global address book, 65
Go To Source command, 174
Grant Permissions button, 142
Grant Permissions dialog box, 145
group calendars, 57
group conversations, 100–108
    desktop, sharing, 101–102
    instant message conversations, 112–115
    online polls, 107–108
    presentations, sharing, 102–105
    presenters and attendees, 101
    programs, sharing, 106–107
    starting, 100–101
    subject, changing, 129
    taking notes on, 128–129
    video feeds, 115–116
    whiteboards, sharing, 108
groups, contact, 68–70
    creating, 70
    editing and managing, 119
    joining, 83
    leaving, 83
    in Lync, 117–119
    public groups, 69–71
Groups page, 83
groups (SharePoint), 141–146
    adding users, 145
    creating, 144–145
    site permissions, 142–143
Group Work Site template, 151

H

help and support, 18–26
    community forums, 22–23
    context-sensitive help, 20–21
    how-to procedures and solutions, 24–26
    team blogs, 23
    technical support, 24
    tutorials, 21–22
Help button, 19
Help content
    context-sensitive, 20–21
    printing and sharing, 21
Help For Admins, 19
home page, 4–9
    Ask A Question In The Forums link, 22
    Community links, 7–8
    Help button, 19
    My Profile link, 17
    navigation bar, 5–6

home page (*Continued*)
  Outlook link, 11
  panes, 5
  Participate In The Community link, 22
  resource links, 6
  Resources list, 12
  search box, 18
  Shared Documents link, 15
  small business edition, 15
  Start Here section, 21
  Team Site link, 13
Home wiki page, 180
How To Import Your Contacts link, 71
how-to procedures, 24–26
How To Use This Library page, 180
Hyperlink dialog box, 84

I
ID for sign-in, 4
Ignore Conversation command, 39, 41
I Like It button, 138
images
  adding to shared presentations, 104
  attaching to e-mail messages, 35
Import Contacts dialog box, 71
importing contacts, 71
import spreadsheet lists, 183
Import Your Contacts From An Existing E-Mail
    Account shortcut, 71
inbox rules, 45–50
  action words or phrases, 47
  basis of, 46, 48
  creating, 45–49
  managing, 48–50
information management policy settings, list, 185
inline editing, 158
instant messages, 6, 112–115
  attachments in, 114
  background color, 92
  calls and e-mail messages, responding with,
    113–115
  continuing conversation, 124
  conversation history, 99
  fonts, 92
  formatting, 92, 113
  groups, sending to, 113
  multiple conversations, 112–113
  redirecting, 115
  responding to, 112
  sending, 114
  sharing content in, 113
Internet Explorer 9 notification bar, 44
Issues Web Database template, 153
issue-tracking lists, 183
item limits, 158

J
Junk E-Mail folder, 88
junk e-mail, managing, 88–90

K
Keep Me Signed In option, 5
keywords, 185

L
Learn How To Manually Configure Outlook link, 10
libraries, 14. *See also* document libraries
  columns, creating, 159–161
  connecting, 179
  content type settings, 165
  creating, 154–156
  customizing, 178
  document libraries, 166–179
  documents, checking out and in, 164, 172–173
  documents, copying from, 173–174
  documents, uploading to, 32
  exporting, 179
  filtering, 158
  inline editing, 158
  notes and tags, adding, 137
  offline access, 179
  settings, managing, 161–165
  Share & Track group, 170–172
  shortcuts in Office applications, 179
  types of, 154–155
  version management, 164–165, 173
  views, 156–159
  wiki page libraries, 180–181
  workflow settings, 161–164
Library Settings page, 161–191
linking wiki pages
  , 180
links lists, 183
lists, 14, 182–189
  appearance, changing, 149
  creating, 183
  forms, 149–150
  general settings, 184
  items, adding, 185–186
  items, editing, 186
  notes and tags, adding, 137
  offline access to, 189
  permissions and management settings, 185
  RSS feeds, sending as, 185
  settings, 184–185
  surveys, 187–189
  task lists, 187
  types of, 182–183
  views, 149
  workflows, 185

List Settings page, 184–185
list templates, 147, 183, 185
local senders, 89
location setting, 122
logging, configuration options, 93
Lync Attendee, 110
Lync Online, 91–130
   32-bit and 64-bit versions, 7
   Activities Feed list, 123
   Always On Top option, 128
   audio conferencing, 115
   capabilities, 6, 91
   configuration options, 91–100
   contacts, managing, 117–125
   conversations, 123–126, 129
   file saving information, 98
   group conversations, 100–108
   installing, 7–8
   instant messages, 112–115
   language settings, 92
   location information, 94
   minimizing to notification area, 93
   My Account area, 93
   OneNote, taking notes in, 128–129
   online meetings, 109–112
   Personal Information Manager settings, 93
   presence information, 121–123
   Recording Manager, 126–127
   sign-in e-mail address, 93
   signing in to, 7
   stage, 101, 105–107
   status information, 121–123
   Tools menu, 91
   video conferences, 115–116
Lync Recording Player, 126–127
Lync window, 7
   Welcome To Lync link, 22

M

mailbox folders, filtering messages in, 42
Mail Merge wizard. *See* mail merge
Mail Setup dialog box, 109
Mail view, 33–50
   navigating in, 27–28
Manage Categories dialog box, 61
Manage Copies command, 174
Manage My Alerts command, 171
Manage Permissions command, 169
Mark Complete command, 77–78
meeting organizers, 53
meeting requests, 52–54
   attendees, selecting, 55
   automatic processing, 86
   busy and free information, 55
   date and time information, 55
   meeting information, 52–53
   notifications, 85
   regularly occurring meetings, 53
   reminders, 62
   replies, 53
   responding to, 53–54
   Scheduling Assistant for, 55–56
   sending, 52–53, 109
meetings, online. *See* online meetings
Meetings templates, 152
Meet Now command, 100
merging documents. *See* mail merge
messages. *See* e-mail; instant messages; Outlook
      Web App
metadata navigation settings, 184
Microsoft Access, with SharePoint sites, 152
Microsoft Certification ID, ix
Microsoft Certified Professional website, ix
Microsoft Customer Experience Improvement
      Program, 92
Microsoft LifeCam, 98
Microsoft Lync. *See* Lync Online
Microsoft Lync Recording Manager, 126–127
Microsoft Office. *See* Office desktop applications
Microsoft Office Professional Plus, installing, 9
Microsoft Office Specialist Expert (MOS Expert)
   Microsoft Office Specialist Expert (MOS Expert)
      defined , vii
   Microsoft Office Specialist Expert (MOS Expert)
      expectations , viii
Microsoft Office Specialist (MOS)
   Microsoft Office Specialist (MOS)defined , vii
   Microsoft Office Specialist (MOS)expectations , viii
Microsoft Office Specialist program
   Microsoft Office Specialist programbenefits of, ix
   Microsoft Office Specialist programcertification
      path, choosing , vii
   Microsoft Office Specialist programcertification
      paths, listed, vii
   Microsoft Office Specialist programexams,
      described, x
   Microsoft Office Specialist programexam time
      limit, viii
   Microsoft Office Specialist programexam tips, viii
   Microsoft Office Specialist programlogo,
      personalizing, x
   Microsoft Office Specialist programobjective
      domain, viii
Microsoft OneNote, 128–129
Microsoft Online Services ID, 4–5
Microsoft Online Services Sign-in Assistant,
      installing, 7
Microsoft Outlook. *See* Outlook; Outlook Web App
Microsoft SharePoint. *See* SharePoint Online

Microsoft Support site Office 365 page, 24
mobile access to libraries, 159
mobile phones
  notifications, receiving on, 85, 87, 88
  Outlook Web App settings, 86–88
Mobile Phone Setup Reference link, 87
Modify Form Web Parts button, 149
MOS 2010 Study Guide for Microsoft Office
    SharePoint e-book, 131
Multipage Meeting Workspace template, 152
My Calendars, 29
My Contacts, 29
My Content, 140
My Profile, 16–17, 139
  colleagues, adding, 140
  editing, 139
My Site, 139–141
  My Content page, 140
  tag cloud, 138
  tags and notes, 137
My Site profile
  categories, 139
  updating, 141
My Tasks, 30

N

Navigate Up icon, 32
navigating
  applications, 26–32
  with breadcrumbs, 32
  in Calendar view, 28–29
  in Contacts view, 29–30
  in Mail view, 27–28
  Office 365 features, 3–26
  with Quick Launch, 31–32
  in Tasks view, 30
  team site, 30–32
navigation pane (Outlook Web App), 26–30
New Account Creation Wizard, 79
New Alert dialog box, 170
New Document command, 166–167
New Document Library page, 166
New Folder dialog box, 167
New Group window, 69
New Inbox Rule dialog box, 47
  More Options link, 47
  When The Message Arrives, And option, 48
New Item dialog box, 185–186
New Message To Contact command, 66
New Page dialog box, 180
Newsfeeds area, 139
New Task Item window, 73–75
note board, 137

notes, 136–138
  adding, 137
  in OneNote, 128–129
notification bar in e-mail message window, 36
notifications
  automatic processing, 86
  configuration settings, 96
  on document changes, 170–171
  mobile phone, receiving on, 85, 87, 88
  on giving or requesting control over desktop, 101

O

objective domain
  objective domainin MOS exams, viii
Office 365
  accessibility settings, 86
  help and support, 18–26
  information about, 8
  Office desktop applications, configuring for, 9–11
  quick-start guide, 21
  small business edition, 15–16
  Start menu shortcut, 10
Office365.com, 8–9
Office 365 community, 22–23
Office 365 e-mail account, setting up, 109
Office 365 Technical Blog, 23
Office desktop applications
  coauthoring documents, 177
  configuring for Office 365, 9–11
  library shortcuts, adding, 179
offline access to team site content, 179, 189–192
Offline status, 122
Off Work status, 122
OneNote, 128–129
online meetings, 6, 109–112
  access and presenters options, 109
  admitting attendees, 110–111
  joining, 112
  leaving and ending, 112
  notes in OneNote, 128–129
  presenters, 110
  recording, 98, 111, 112, 126–127
  saving settings, 110
  scheduling, 112
  starting, 110
online polls, 107–108
Open In Browser command, 44
opinion polls, 107–108
Options dialog box (Lync)
  Alerts page, 96
  Audio Device page, 97
  File Saving page, 98
  General page, 92–93

Options dialog box (Lync) (*Continued*)
My Picture page, 94–95
opening, 91, 98
Personal page, 93–94
Phones page, 95–96
Ringtones And Sounds page, 96–97
Status page, 94
Video Device page, 97–98
Options window (Outlook Web App)
calendar settings, 64
Create An Inbox Rule option, 45–46
Phone page, 87
Settings page, 83
Organize E-Mail page
Automatic Replies page, 80–81
Delivery Reports page, 81
Retention Policies page, 82
Other Calendars group, 60
Other Contacts group, 117, 118
Outlook
compatibility with Outlook Web App, 6
configuring to work with Office 365, 10–11
exporting contacts to Outlook Web App, 71
libraries, connecting to, 179
Office 365 e-mail account in, 109
and Outlook Web App, connecting, 6
SharePoint task list, connecting, 187
Outlook Options page Account view, 12
Outlook Web App, 11–13, 33–90
Accessibility settings, 86
account options, 78–80
Actions menu, 40–41
Calendar link, 11–12
Calendar view, 28–29, 50–64
categories, 60–61
configuring, 11, 78–90
connected accounts, 79–80
contacts, importing, 71
Contacts view, 29–30, 65–72
and desktop version, connecting, 6
e-mail, blocking and allowing messages, 88–90
e-mail folders, managing, 27–28
e-mail, managing, 33–50
Favorites list, 27–28
Filter menu, 41
flags, 61–62
groups options, 83
Help pages, 21–22
Inbox link, 11–12
language and time zone, 12
Mail view, 27–28
message list, 37–38
mobile phones, working with, 86–88
navigation pane, 26–30
Options link, 11–12
Organize E-Mail, 80–82

Outlook settings, 83–86
reading pane, 37–38
Regional Settings, 86
reminders, 62–63
search box, 42–44
starting, 12–13
Tasks view, 30, 73
views, 11, 26

P

Page History button, 180
pages, adding to team site, 181–182
Participate In The Community link, 22
passwords
changing, 17–18
for sign-in, 4
strong, 4
People Options button, 100, 113
People's Calendars group, 57, 60
People searches, 133
per-location view settings, list, 184
permissions
defining, 143
list, 185
for SharePoint features, 14
on SharePoint sites, 131, 142–144
on subsites, 150
personal address books, 65
Personal Information Manager, 93
Personalization Site template, 151
personal SharePoint sites, 139–141
phones
secondary ringer, 97
synchronizing with Outlook, 87
photographs
of contacts, 94–95
My Picture, displaying, 94–95, 99
in profile, 17–18
picture libraries, 155
polls, online, 107–108
portal.microsoftonline.com, 4–5
portal page, 3. *See also* **home page**
accessing, 4–5
displaying, 7
Office365.com, signing in with, 8–9
opening, 4–9
PowerPoint presentations
annotating, 103, 104
drawing in, 103
full screen viewing, 104
images, adding, 104
pointing to objects, 103
saving with annotations, 104
sharing, 102–105
thumbnail images, 104

presence information, 51
  configuration settings, 94
  displaying, 6
  managing, 121–123
  of privacy relationships, 121
privacy relationships, 93, 119–121
  for contacts, 118
  phone information and, 95
  presence information, 121
private views, 157–158
procedures, help and support, 24–26
profile
  Information area, 16
  My Site profile, 139–141
  password, changing, 17–18
  photographs in, 17–18
  updating, 16–18
programs, sharing, 106–107
Projects Web Database template, 153
project tasks lists, 183
public groups (contacts), 69–71
  joining, 83
public views, 157–158
publishing
  calendars, 58–60
  documents, 176–177
  recordings, 127
Publish Major Version dialog box, 176
Publish This Calendar To Internet command, 58

Q

Quick Launch, 31–32
  document workspaces, 175
  Site Pages link, 31
  wiki pages in, 180
quick-start guide, 21

R

rating settings, 184
reading pane (Outlook Web App), 37
  attachments, viewing, 44
  configurations options, 84–85
  positioning, 38
Read permission, 142
read receipts, 84
real-time communications. *See* Lync Online
recorded meetings, 111
Recording Manager, 126–127
  opening, 126
recordings
  managing, 126–127
  publishing, 127
  save location, 98

Recycle Bin link, 31
Redirect button, 114
Regional Settings (Outlook), 86
relationships with contacts, 119–121. *See also* privacy relationships
reminders
  for appointments, 51
  configuration settings, 86
  responding to, 62–63
  setting, 62–64
  turning off, 62
repeating tasks, 75–76
  marking as complete, 77
Repetition dialog box, 75, 76
Reply All button, 40
Reply button, 40
Reply With Instant Message command, 114
report libraries, 155
Request Control command, 101
resource links, 6
retention policies, 82
Retention Policies page, 82
ringtones, configuration options, 96–97, 99
RSS feeds, sending lists as, 185

S

Safe Senders And Recipients list, 89
Save And Publish Options dialog box, 127
Save List As Template command, 147
Save Site As Template command, 146
Scheduling Assistant, 55–56
scroll bars (Word), 2
search box
  for help and support, 7, 18
  Outlook Web App, 42–44
searching
  advanced searches, 43–44, 133–135
  by category, 60
  contacts, 72, 118–119
  e-mail messages, 42–44
  query syntax, 132
  scope, changing, 43–44
  scope, setting, 132–133
  search results, refining, 135–136
  for site content, 132–136
  tags and, 138
search results page, 18–19
Search templates, 152
search terms, 138
secondary ringers, 97
See Also paragraphs, xi
Select Members dialog box, 70
Select Owner dialog box, 70
Send An Instant Message command, 112

Send An Instant Message To button, 114
Send To command, 175
Set Alert On This Document command, 172
Set Your Location box, 122
shared address book, 65
shared content, managing, 105–106
Shared Documents library, 175
Shared Documents link, 15, 32
SharePoint Online, 131–192
  groups, 141–146
  Help pages, 21–22
  libraries, 154–156
  managing site content, 154–191
  managing sites, 136–153
  My Site profile, 139–141
  searching for content, 132–136
  site permissions, 131
  team site, 13
SharePoint Online Administration Center, 184
SharePoint sites. *See also* team sites
  adding users, 145
  list templates, 147
  managing, 136–153
  note board, 137
  permissions on, 142–144
  personal sites, 139–141
  tags and notes, 136–138
SharePoint team sites, 131. *See also* team sites
SharePoint Workspace 2010, 189–190
Share PowerPoint dialog box, 102–103
Share Programs dialog box, 106
Share Site command, 141
Share This Calendar command, 56
Share & Track group, 170–172
Share Your SharePoint Site dialog box, 141
sharing
  calendars, 56–58
  content from stage, 105
  desktop, 101–102
  permissions on, 57–58
  PowerPoint presentations, 102–105
  programs, 106–107
  team sites, 141
  whiteboards, 108
signatures, e-mail, 35
  adding, 84
signing in, authentication credentials for, 4
Sign In link, 8
sign-in page, 4
Site Actions menu
  Edit Page page, 149, 178
  More Options command, 180
  New Document Library page, 166

New Site page, 150
Share Site command, 141
Site Settings page, 132, 142, 146
Sync To SharePoint Workspace command, 189
site content
  managing, 154–191
  searching for, 132–136
  working with offline, 189–190
Site Pages library, 182
Site Pages link, 31
site permissions, 131
Site Settings page, 132, 142, 146
site templates
  creating, 146–147
  for subsites, 150
Site Theme page, 148
site themes, 148–149
slide libraries, 155
small business edition of Office 365, 15–16
  team site and website, 15–16
  three-state workflows, 14
Snipping Tool, 95
Social Meeting Workspace template, 152
Solutions gallery, site templates in, 146
solutions, step-by-step, 24–26
sorting
  document libraries, 175–176
  library views, 158
sounds, configuration options, 96–97, 99
source documents, links to, 174
spelling checker, for e-mail messages, 36, 85
stage (Lync), 101
  shared content record, 105
  sharing content from, 105–107
  tools in, 103
Start A Conference Call command, 115
Start A Video Call command, 115
Start menu, Office 365 shortcut on, 10
status lists, 183
status settings
  configuration of, 94
  managing, 121–123
  manually changing, 122
strong passwords, 4
subsites, 14
  creating, 150–154
  permissions on, 150
  site templates for, 150
support, technical, 18–26
surveys, 183, 187–188
Sync To SharePoint Workspace command, 179, 189

T

tabular views, 158
tag cloud, 138, 140
tags, 136–138
  adding, 137–138
Tags & Notes button, 137
Take Back Control command, 101
Take Notes Using OneNote command, 128
task list (Outlook Web App), 73, 75–76
task lists (SharePoint), 183, 187
tasks
  attachments to, 74
  categories, 61
  completed, 77–78
  % Complete value, 76
  creating, 73–76
  Deferred status, 74
  due dates, 73
  flagging items, 61–62
  managing, 73
  priority of, 74
  private, 77
  reminders for, 63, 77
  repeating, 75–76
  status information, 74, 76
  updating, 76–77
Tasks folder, 30
Tasks list, 187
Tasks view, 73
  navigating in, 30
team blogs, 23
Team Discussion list, 188
Team Site Members group, 141–142
  adding users, 145
Team Site Owners group, 141–142
team sites, 131–192. *See also* **SharePoint sites**
  advanced searches, 133–135
  basic pages, 181–182
  content, managing, 154–191
  creating, 150–153
  discussion boards, 188–189
  document libraries, 14
  Getting Started topics, 22
  groups and permissions, 141–146
  lists, 14
  managing, 136–153
  navigating, 30–32
  opening in new window, 13
  pages, adding, 31, 181–182
  searching for content, 132–136
  search scope settings, 132–133
  sharing, 141
  site owners, 142
  site templates, creating, 146–147
  small business edition, 15–16

  subsites, 14, 150–154
  syncing to SharePoint Workspace, 189–190
  themes, applying, 148–149
  three-state workflows, 14
  users, adding, 13
  viewing, 13–16
  wiki page libraries, 180–181
  working offline with content, 189–192
Team Site template, 151
Team Site Visitors group, 141
technical support, 24
technology certification, benefits of, vii
templates
  list, 147, 183, 185
  site, 146–147, 151–153
  workflow, 162
terms, search, 138
text
  textselecting (Word). *See* also selecting (Word)
text message notifications, 85, 87, 88
themes, site, 148–149
three-state workflows, 14, 162
Tip paragraphs, xi
To and Cc lines, 34
to-do lists, managing, 73–78
troubleshooting tool, 25–26
tutorials, 21–22

U

Unknown status, 122
Unpublish command, 177
updates, installing, 10
Upload Document command, 168
uploading documents, 168
Upload Multiple Documents dialog box, 168
Use Conversations command, 39, 41
users
  external, sharing team site with, 141
  site permissions, 142–144
Use The Blind And Low Vision Experience option,
    86

V

validation settings, column, 184
Version History dialog box, 169, 173
versioning settings, 164–165, 176, 184
versions, managing, 173
video conferences, 115–116
video devices, configuration options, 97–98
View All Pages command, 180
View Conversation History command, 123, 125
View Only permission, 142
View Properties command, 169

views
  columns in, 157
  creating, 159
  custom columns in, 161
  editing, 159
  folderless, 158
  grouping items, 158
  inline editing, 158
  item limits, 158
  library views, 156–159
  mobile settings, 159
  personal or public, 157–158
  sort columns, 158
  summary information, 158
  tabular, 158
Visio Process Repository template, 151
Voice over Internet Protocol (VoIP), 115
volume, configuration options, 97

W

webcams, configuration settings, 97–98, 115
web conferences, 109–112
Web Databases templates, 152
web pages, adding notes and tags, 137
web part pages
  adding to team site, 181–182
  editing, 149
  layout, 181
web parts
  adding to pages, 178
  appearance, changing, 149

web part zones, 181
Welcome To Lync link, 22
whiteboards, sharing, 108
wiki page libraries, 155, 180–181
  linking to pages, 180
wiki pages
  editing, 180
  version history, 180
  viewing all, 180
Windows Media recordings, 126
Windows Photo Editor, 95
Word
  checking in documents, 172
  coauthoring documents, 177
workflows
  actions, 163
  defining, 162
  settings, 161–164, 185
  starting, 163
  three-state, 14
Workflow Settings page, 162–164
Workgroup contacts, 120
working offline with team site content, 189–192
worksheets
  coauthoring, 177
  from task lists, 187

X

XPS files, 104

About the Author

John Pierce was an editor and writer at Microsoft Corporation for 12 years. He is now a freelance editor and writer who frequently works on books and articles related to Microsoft software and technologies. He is the author or coauthor of *MOS 2010 Study Guide for Microsoft Word Expert, Excel Expert, Access, and SharePoint*; *MOS 2010 Study Guide for Microsoft OneNote Exam*; *Microsoft Office Groove 2007 Step by Step*; *Microsoft Access 2003 Inside Track*; and *Microsoft Small Business Kit*.

What do you think of this book?

We want to hear from you!
To participate in a brief online survey, please visit:

microsoft.com/learning/booksurvey

Tell us how well this book meets your needs—what works effectively, and what we can do better. Your feedback will help us continually improve our books and learning resources for you.

Thank you in advance for your input!